ROUGHING IT EASY

Brigham Young University Press
Provo, Utah

ROUGHING IT EASY

A Unique Ideabook for Camping and Cooking

Dian Thomas

Library of Congress Cataloging in Publication Data
Thomas, Dian, 1945-
  Roughing it easy; A unique ideabook for camping and cooking.
  1. Outdoor cookery. 2. Camping. I. Title.
TX823.T48   641.5'78   73-22348
ISBN 0-8425-0887-2
ISBN 0-8425-0892-9 (pbk.)

Library of Congress Catalog Card Number: 73-22348
International Standard Book Number: 0-8425-0887-2 (hardback)
                                  0-8425-0892-9 (paperback)
Brigham Young University Press, Provo, Utah 84602
© 1974 Brigham Young University Press. All rights reserved
Second printing 1974
Printed in the United States of America
74 25M 5948

For
Julian Thomas, my father

CONTENTS

Foreword   ix

Preface   xi

1   Introduction   1

2   Planning   5

3   Campsite   21

4   Fire Building   41

5   Methods of Cooking   55

6   Recipes   115

7   Sourdough   183

8   First Aid   189

Colorplates   149

Index   199

FOREWORD

Enjoyment and adventure in the outdoors are within reach of nearly every American. Two of the most popular and pleasant activities that occur under open skies are camping and cooking. Whether it be on the patio, in the backyard, in the park, or in distant places of beauty and solitude — the outdoors enhances the fun of sleeping, cooking, and eating. In this book Dian Thomas has helped make outdoor learning and living quality experiences and has contributed greatly to an important but often overlooked aspect of outdoor education.

The author's expertise in her professional field of home economics education and her interest in outdoor education are reflected by the broad scope of this book. The importance of the multidisciplinary approach to outdoor education is aptly illustrated by the role which outdoor cooking plays in camping, exploring, backpacking, picnicking, and other forms of outdoor adventure. It is hoped that many others in Dian's field of education will become interested and involved in outdoor education programs in their own institutions.

Camping and outdoor cooking and the many concomitant experiences associated with them not only add energy and vitality to the body — they refresh the mind and feed the soul.

Julian W. Smith
Professor, College of Education,
Michigan State University;
and Director, Outdoor Education Project,
American Association for Health,
Physical Education, and Recreation

Editorial Comment: This book is designed to take you step by step through the planning stages of your outdoor adventure, from explicit directions on how to set up economical and useful camp quarters to menu planning, shopping, and the preparation of specific meals. The excitement of adding interest and variety to cooking makes outdoor living a creative and challenging experience.

Dian Thomas, a successful and acclaimed teacher in both the Home Economics Education Department and the Food Science and Nutrition Department at Brigham Young University, is one of the first in her field to include outdoor cooking in the home economics classroom. Having served as director of the Brighton MIA (Mutual Improvement Association) camp for two summers and as program director and counselor for five, Dian brings a solid background of camping experience to the units of outdoor education she has taught not only in junior high school but also on the BYU campus and on education-week tours throughout Canada and the United States. In her education classes she has adapted outdoor methods to principles of cooking taught in schools across the country — methods that lend sparkle and excitement to food preparation in the classroom.

But the most important classroom for this text is the out-of-doors. This book, utilizing Dian's creative ideas and practical knowledge, is written for anyone who is interested in camping and cooking. It is a guide to be used not only in the schoolroom but on weekend fishing and camping trips as well.

If you will begin with the chapter on planning and follow Dian's advice throughout the book, you'll find that your outdoor adventures are suddenly more fulfilling and a lot more fun.

PREFACE

Cooking without a kitchen demands some particular skills campers should be able to develop after they understand a few basic facts and have some definite guidelines. This book is designed to present those facts and guidelines in such a way that even the most inexperienced cook will be able to learn how to turn out a delicious outdoor meal or plan an entire camping trip, including a menu for a group.

Beginning with guidelines for planning destination, length of trip, and clothing needs, the book will show you how to set up an outdoor home away from home, how to plan and shop for a complete menu, and how to cook foods using many different methods.

Hints that help make camping easier appear in every section. For example, soaping pans on the outside before putting them on the heat will keep them from blackening. Baking an individual cake inside an orange peel wrapped in foil not only saves dishes but makes the cake taste better. You will learn how to start fires without matches by using batteries and steel wool or a bow drill, and you will learn how to cook two separate dishes in a Dutch oven using aluminum foil dividers.

Charts for planning menus, shopping trips, cooking methods, and budgeting time are some of the most helpful items in the book. You will also be interested in the substitute list — what foods can be substituted for other items in an emergency. For school home economics classes in outdoor education, or as guides for group camping trips, the section on work division will be helpful.

You will find tested recipes and methods of cooking, along with clear instructions and illustrations that will help make your camping fun. And, hopefully, after you master these skills, you will use the principles outlined to help you create ideas of your own.

Producing a work such as this requires more than just the author's expertise. My father, for example, who learned as a youthful sheepherder to make sourdough and who baked bread and rolls under the open skies for my mother-to-be, contributed the chapter on sourdough. Mary McConkie Donoho supplemented my knowledge of first aid to help build that chapter into one with greater substance. Marilyn Miller and Gloria Stratton provided valuable assistance in organizing and compiling the manuscript. William Whitaker supplied the line drawings and Stan MacBean the photographs. Louise Hanson and Carole Wade collaborated as editor and designer to smooth the whole into the finished product. I thank especially not only everyone who contributed ideas and encouragement but also the students who participated with me in the outdoor experiences which led to the creation of this book.

INTRODUCTION

Living outdoors has become a favorite American pastime, almost reaching the dimension of sports. Learning to use the skills and the imagination to cope with the inconveniences of the natural environment has become a challenge to American families, youth groups, students, and teachers. Inherent in outdoor living are opportunities for everyone to build human relationships, to find satisfying outlets for creative energy, and to enjoy relaxation in leisure time.

One of the best ways to get to know another person is to work closely with him in outdoor activity. While one person gathers the wood for the fire, another breaks or stacks the tinder. One person prepares the meat while another prepares the onions for the foil dinner. Opportunities present themselves for giving and taking, sharing services, exchanging pleasant conversation.

As an activity for a family, an outing is a perfect affair. From the first stages of planning until its completion, an outing allows every family member to participate. One large family I know carefully organizes every detail following the plans in this book. They decide together in a democratic way when and where they will go, and then they choose a historian and a photographer to record the event, a chief menu-planner, a shopper, and other leaders according to their needs. Together they sit down and decide what kind of food they will have at each meal, giving and taking where there are particular likes or dislikes. When the menu is planned, the chief shopper makes a complete list, and everyone goes shopping. The chief equipment engineer has the cooperation of family members in packing the equipment, and the family is off to the mountains for a fun-filled, outdoor time.

As a teacher and group leader at camp, I have seen what can happen when groups of young people plan for an outdoor event. There is immediate excitement, rapport, and cooperation — and a sense of pride and self-fulfillment. The experience builds confidence and character.

One eighth-grade girl who at one time defied my authority in the classroom changed her attitude completely on a cookout. The classroom experience had seemed to threaten her — she seemed rebellious, a troublemaker, unable to cope with competition or grades. But on the cookout, as the chief in charge of preparing the dessert, she found immediate success. I showed her how to prepare it, and she did the rest. She was proud of her work. The successful experience boosted her self-concept. Our relationship improved.

The possibilities for young people to achieve success with creative outdoor experiences are limitless. The out-of-doors is a perfect place for them to learn cooking skills. Their inexperienced hands do not need to worry about clumsiness, accidents, or dirt. They love the informality, the feel of the fresh air, and the taste of food cooked over the coals.

However, not only young people but people of all ages enjoy the feelings of teamwork and creativity that come from participating together in outdoor activities. Several weeks after one of my demonstrations I talked with a woman in her early fifties who had been present. She shared with me her excitement about her last few weekends. An administrator and a writer in a busy office, she and her husband, who also worked under administrative and teaching pressures, had grown weary of trying to accomplish any-thing at home on the weekends. "We were constantly interrupted by the telephone and by business associates dropping in," she said. "We decided to take some of your outdoor tips, along with our materials for studying and writing, and head for the mountains."

She described how they had built a star fire, which she had learned to do from my demonstration, slowly pushing the logs toward the center. "We sat beside the fire, writing and studying — taking time out to make 's'mores' over the coals and to just chat." That was the first weekend. The next weekend they made ham-burgers on a tin-can stove they had fashioned themselves. "When we left," she told me, "we did everything you had told us to do to put out the fire, stirring and watering the coals, digging them under, and leaving everything as if no one had been there. We felt a real kinship with nature."

But the most rewarding consequence of their weekend outdoor trips was their discovery that they really enjoy being together. "Finding time for each other has been difficult in the past," she confessed. "Now we make it a point to run away together every weekend we can — like truant schoolchildren discovering nature's wonders and relishing every moment of it."

Time after time I have seen how thrilling it is for people to start a fire in some new way or create some new outdoor dish, to watch their sourdough biscuits turn out beautifully, to wait with mouths watering to taste the barbecued chicken turned to a golden brown over the spit, or to turn out a sugar-glazed pineapple upside-down-cake from a big Dutch oven.

And year after year I am often visited by campers who remember the experiences we had some summer of perhaps ten years ago — girls for whom the camping experience was a highlight in their lives. Out there in the great outdoors they weren't under the influence of pressures or fads. Their minds were open to new ideas, their lives subject to reflection and creative experience, their days filled with memorable occasions. They often ask me, "Do you remember the biscuits that we almost burned on the hike to the lake?" "Do you remember how we cleaned the fish we caught in Bear River?" "Do you remember when we climbed to the top of Mount Majestic to watch the sunrise?"

After a climb into the thin, vast blueness that tastes so fresh on the tongue, we would often sit and look out over the valleys below us that sometimes stretched untrampled for miles. We would talk about our lives.

"See those mountains out there?" I would say; "Think of them as the mountain peaks of your life. Each one is a challenge to climb. But remember you have climbed this one, and you can climb every one of them in the same way."

We set goals; we molded character; we found new challenges for living.

It seems to me the outdoor experience is one of the essential experiences of life, and my hope is that some of the ideas I offer here will help to enrich that experience for everyone.

PLANNING

The first ingredient of a successful outing is a good plan. Consideration should be made of time, destination, activities, food, personal equipment, and organizing group tasks. This chapter is designed to give you basic information and helpful ideas on all those things which you need to do before the actual camping experience. Use it to help in making your preliminary trip decisions.

Time

All the other preplanning for a trip, of course, depends on the allotted time you have. Will the trip be just for the morning or afternoon; will it be for overnight, for a weekend, or longer? Backpacking trips and long camping trips will take more careful planning than an evening cookout.

Destination

Your destination will be a factor determining how carefully you plan the trip. Considerations of climate and length of trip dictate the amount of clothing you will need. You should make careful purchases for locations where shopping is impossible. More clothing will be needed for colder areas. Drinking water may have to be transported to areas where no water is available. As much pertinent information as possible should be gathered about the selected destination so that accurate planning and preparation can be made.

Activities

It is important that you organize each day's activities, then plan the equipment, clothing, and meals around them. A long afternoon hike, for example, will allow just enough time for a one-pot meal to simmer on the coals. For an all-day hike, on the other hand, plan a hearty breakfast, a simple sack lunch carried in a day pack or sack around the belt, and a snack for energy; and if you intend to be late returning to camp, plan a meal requiring short preparation or a meal that has already been prepared and left to cook while you are away.

After making the above decisions, you are now ready to consider clothing and food and to organize the responsibilities of each camper.

Food

Plan simple, well-balanced meals; then shop carefully, purchasing only those items you will use. For more help in planning foods and to be sure of well-balanced and interesting meals, refer to the chapter in this book on recipes.

Clothing

Plan clothing which will give protection and warmth while allowing freedom for activities. Take only the essentials.

Shoes

Among the first items to consider are shoes. They are especially important if you plan to hike. Choose a sturdy, comfortable pair which will give support and protection. Avoid tennis shoes since they give neither. Avoid wearing new shoes to remain free from foot discomfort and blisters.

Socks

Lightweight socks are good to wear around camp, but for hiking, wool socks are best because they absorb moisture and cushion the feet. Wearing two pairs of socks during a hike — a light pair under a heavier pair — will help prevent blister-causing friction. Or carry bandaids and tape them over areas rubbed by your shoes before these areas have a chance to blister.

Pants

Long, sturdy pants will provide protection from branches, sharp rocks, sunburn, fire, or hot cooking grease. Tight-fitting pants restrain freedom and should be avoided.

Shirt

Long sleeves provide the best protection against sunburn, insects, and evening coolness.

Hat

A hat will give some protection against the sun.

Jacket

A water-repellent jacket is best, but either a plastic bag or a square of plastic can be improvised for use as a poncho.

The plastic is lightweight and easy to carry.

Coat

A warm coat is a welcome relief from night and early morning chill in some areas.

Sleeping Equipment

The most essential item for a good night's rest is a warm sleeping bag. If you suspect that the bag will not be warm enough, take additional blankets. When a sleeping bag is not available, make a bedroll: lay a tarp on the ground and spread one blanket over it. Lay the outside edge of a second blanket down the center of the first so that it is halfway off the first. Lay a third blanket over the first and a fourth blanket over the second. If you desire more blankets, continue in the same manner. And if you desire a sheet, lay it down as the last blanket. To close the bedroll, take the outside edge of the top blanket and bring it to its other edge. Continue overlapping blankets until the bedroll is completely folded. To close the bottom, fold it under three inches and pin it in several places (fig. 1).

Take a pair of warm pajamas. You will sleep warmer and more comfortably if you do not sleep in the clothes you have been wearing all day. Cool nights make warm pajamas and wool socks welcome items.

A ground cloth is essential to keep sleeping bags clean and free from ground moisture. An air mattress or foam pad will also protect against ground moisture as well as against the hardness and lumpiness of the ground.

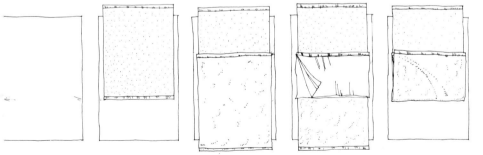

Fig. 1. Bedroll

Personal Equipment List

The following is a suggested personal equipment list for extended camping trips. Blanks are provided for planning the number of each item needed, determined by the length of stay.

Clothing
_____ Coat
_____ Hat
_____ Jacket, sweater, or
       sweatshirt
_____ Pants (long)
_____ Rain equipment
_____ Shirts
_____ Shoes (two pair: one
       for hiking)
_____ Socks (light)
_____ Socks (wool)
_____ Underclothing

Sleeping equipment
_____ Air mattress or foam
       pad
_____ Ground cloth
_____ Pajamas (warm)
_____ Pillow
_____ Sleeping bag or
       bedroll

Personal items
_____ Comb
_____ Mirror
_____ Mosquito repellent
_____ Suntan lotion
_____ Toothbrush and
       toothpaste
_____ Towel
_____ Wash cloth

Miscellaneous
_____ Camera and film
_____ Chapstick
_____ First-aid kit

_____ Flashlight
_____ Medicine (teacher or
        leader should be
        informed of special
        medication needs)
_____ Money (maximum
        amount $_____)
_____ Musical instrument
_____ Pocket knife
_____ Sun glasses

General Camping Equipment

When you plan your camping trip, the safety and accessibility of the area and the length of stay should be considered before you plan what equipment to take. An area you drive to will allow more pieces of equipment than one you pack in to. An afternoon cook-out will require less equipment than a week's stay.

Two suggestions to remember when you consider equipment are these: (1) take as little as possible; (2) take equipment that can be used in many different ways and then discarded, such as cans and foil.

Basic equipment

Some basic pieces of equipment you might need are these: a hatchet or an axe and a blade saw or a string saw. A saw can be faster for cutting wood than an axe, especially for those who are not skilled in using an axe.

For trips that last overnight or longer, tarps, ground cloths, or ponchos are handy. They can be placed under sleeping equipment, used to cover wood piles (especially when it rains) or as a shelter if needed.

Fire equipment

A shovel and some kind of water bucket are very important if open fires are planned. Keep them close to the fire in case the fire spreads.

Another important item of equipment to consider is a pair of asbestos gloves. They are helpful for setting pans on and removing them from the fire; for removing coals, aluminum packages, or hot wood from the fire; or for clearing the coals off the top of a Dutch oven as well as for removing its lid. Use them in any way you would use a hotpad. If asbestos gloves are impossible to purchase, use leather or heavy cotton gloves.

Lighting equipment

Some lighting sources for overnight camping are flashlights and fuel lanterns. If these are not available, a lantern can be built to hold a candle. Cut one end out of a middle-sized or large tin can, punch holes in the top at both ends and thread a wire handle through the holes so that the can is on its side. Either pound a nail upward into the bottom center of the lantern and screw a candle onto the nail or cut a square hole through the tin the same diameter as the candle and screw the end of the candle into the can. Let the bottom of the candle extend below the entrance hole, screwing the candle into the lantern as it burns (fig. 2).

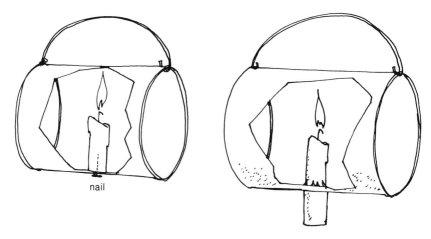

nail

Fig. 2. Tin can lantern

Cooking equipment

The best way to decide what cooking equipment is necessary is to plan menus, then make an itemized equipment list.

Take some basic utensils, at least one good pan or a Dutch oven, and a grill. Improvising many other pieces of equipment is possible.

You can make imaginative use of tin cans, plastic containers, aluminum foil, and sticks. These items are helpful in many ways as utensils and can be discarded at the site. Suggestions for improvising cooking equipment are as follows:

Fig. 3. Tin can rolling pin

- Use a can for a rolling pin (fig. 3).
- Use a can to cut out hamburgers, biscuits, or cookies. Punch a hole in the bottom of the empty can so that air can pass through.
- If you use a can for both cooking and serving food, there are fewer things to clean up.
- A number-ten can can serve as a dishpan.
- Warm vegetables in the cans they come in to save utensils.
- Roll edges of foil around a square made from hanger wire to make a temporary frying pan (fig. 4).
- Deepen a shallow pan with heavy-duty foil (fig. 5).
- Use aluminum foil shaped like a bowl for serving foods (fig. 6).
- Use plastic bags for mixing foods (figs. 7 and 8).
- Use a clean stick as a stirring spoon.
- Cut out side and bottom of plastic bleach bottle and use as a scoop (fig. 9).

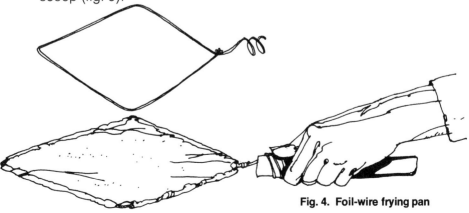

Fig. 4. Foil-wire frying pan

Fig. 5. Pan deepened with foil

Fig. 6. Aluminum foil serving bowl

Fig. 7. Preparing food

Fig. 8. Mixing food in plastic bag

Fig. 9. Scoop made from bleach bottle

Following is a checklist of general camping equipment, kitchen equipment, kitchen supplies, and other miscellaneous equipment for a trip.

Item
_____ Axe
_____ Bucket
_____ Canteen
_____ Compass
_____ Flashlight
_____ Ground cloth
_____ Hatchet
_____ Lantern
_____ Lashing twine
_____ Maps
_____ Packs
_____ Rope (rappelling)
_____ Ropes (small)
_____ Saw
_____ Shovel
_____ String saw
_____ Tent
_____ Tin snips
_____ Whetstone
_____ Wire

Cooking Equipment
_____ Asbestos gloves
_____ Barbecuing equipment
_____ Baking tins
_____ Camp stove
_____ Dutch oven
_____ Grill
_____ Kettles
_____ Mixing bowls
_____ Muffin tin
_____ Reflector oven
_____ Wire rack

Kitchen Tools
_____ Can opener
_____ Knives
_____ Measuring equipment
_____ Peeler
_____ Serving spoons
_____ Spatula
_____ Toasting forks
_____ Turners

Kitchen Supplies
_____ Bar soap
_____ Basic condiments and staples
_____ Charcoal briquets
_____ Dishcloths and towels
_____ Eating utensils
_____ Foil
_____ Garbage bags
_____ Hangers
_____ Lighter fluid
_____ Liquid soap
_____ Matches
_____ Newspapers
_____ Napkins
_____ Paper plates, cups, bowls
_____ Paper towels
_____ Plastic bags
_____ Scrub pads
_____ Soap
_____ Storage containers
_____ Table cover

Group Organization Plan

The key to a successful camping experience is a detailed plan for all the participants. This plan will vary depending on the numbers, sex, and ages of those in the group and the activities already planned. For example, if your first meal at camp is one that has already been cooked, this will give campers more time to unpack and get settled. If campers are involved beforehand in organizing the trip, if they know exactly what needs to be done, and if each of them has chosen a particular assignment for which he will be responsible, everything should run smoothly. Children as well as adults will gain more from the camping experience if they share responsibilities. The following ideas may help in making work assignments.

Trip responsibilities

Everyone should help in some area of the total camping operation.

Group leader: First, choose a group leader who will coordinate all activities and responsibilities.

First-aid assistant: The camp "doctor" or "nurse" arranges first-aid supplies and cares for minor first-aid problems.

Equipment specialist: This person packs the camping equipment, sees that it is properly cared for at camp, and returns each piece to its proper place.

Shopping specialist: Although everyone should help plan and shop for meals, one person should compile the shopping list and organize the shopping.

Photographer: A person especially talented in taking pictures should keep a photographic record of activities.

Journalist: The camp record will be a valuable keepsake for everyone.

Conservation specialist: One person should take the responsibility of seeing that the group sets up conservation standards and keeps them.

Fire specialist: Someone should make sure that all fires are built according to proper safety standards, that they are tended and properly extinguished.

Game chairman: One person should be in charge of planning, organizing, and gathering equipment for games.

Song leader: Sometimes one person will act as song leader

although everyone will join in singing and choosing songs.

Campsite chairman: This person should help the group leader to direct the camp set up and cleanup.

Kitchen specialist: Acting as chef, this person should direct the various campers as each group participates in meal preparation and cleanup.

Meal responsibility

As well as participating in general camp responsibilities, each camper should join in some aspect of meal preparation and cleanup. The following system works very well with a group of six or more who plan to cook at least three meals. Divide the campers into three small groups. Each group will have one of the following duties: (1) fire building, (2) cooking, and (3) cleaning up. The groups will switch duties at each meal until everyone has had the opportunity to be a fire builder, a cook, and a cleanup person.

Fire builders

- Gather and cut plenty of wood for fire.
- Have a shovel and bucket of water on hand in case the fire gets out of control.
- Consult the cooks and build the type of fire they request early enough to allow for ample coals if they are required.
- Keep the fire burning and assign someone to care for it as long as it burns.
- Extinguish the fire.

Cooks

- Tell the fire builders which type of fire is needed and when to start it.
- Plan carefully how much time will be required to cook each item and when its preparation should begin.
- Organize and set up the kitchen.
- Soap the outsides of all kettles to be used in the open fire.
- Prepare and cook all food.

Cleanup

- Prepare a centerpiece and set the table.
- Make sure a grease pit is provided and garbage areas are established.
- Check to see that all food is properly stored.
- When there is room on the fire — hopefully this will be at least

twenty minutes or more before it is time to wash the dishes —
put the dishwater on to heat.
- Prepare the area for dishwashing.
- Put leftover food away.
- Wash all dishes and cooking utensils.
- Make sure that everything in the camp is put away and the camp
  area is cleaned.

Included here is a master planning chart which will help carry
out the above suggestions:

MASTER PLANNING CHART

Trip Planning Leader(s):

Decisions:

Time of stay _____

Dates of trip _____

Destination _____

Persons Going on Trip:

_____

_____

_____

Be Sure to Check:

Things to Consider	Person in Charge	Completed
Trip costs		
Reservations		
Type of transportation		
Route of travel (map)		
Insurance		
Other		

Planning Chairmen: (Fill out own chart below)

Chairman of	Name	Responsibilities
Activities		Plan all activities for trip.
Menus		Check activities; plan all menus around activities.
Equipment		Plan all equipment needs, where to get them, what will be needed.
Meal duties		Organize everybody into small groups to prepare meals and clean up.
Group tasks		Give the entire group specific camp duties.

Chart for Activities Chairman:

Days	Morning	Afternoon	Evening
1			
2			
3			

Chart for Menus Chairman: see chapter on recipes.

Chart for Equipment Chairman:

Kinds of Equipment	Packer	Put Away
Basic camping equipment (see list in planning chapter)		
Kitchen equipment (see list in planning chapter)		
First-aid equipment (see list in first-aid chapter)		
Games — sports		
Arts and crafts		

Chart for Meal Duties Chairman:

Days	Meal	Fire Builders	Cooks	Cleanup
1	breakfast			
	lunch			
	dinner			
2	breakfast			
	lunch			
	dinner			
3	breakfast			
	lunch			
	dinner			

Chart for Group Tasks Chairman:

Duty	Name	Responsibilities
Group leader		Coordinate all activities, responsibilities.
Shopping		Receive menus; compile lists for shopping.
Equipment specialist		Pack, care for, and put away all needed equipment.
Campsite chairman		Help group leader direct set up and cleanup.
Kitchen specialist		Direct groups in meal preparation and cleanup.
Fire specialist		Check fire area; help fire builders in building, tending, extinguishing.
First-aid specialist		Order supplies and give list to shopping chairman, care for minor problems.
Conservation specialist		Help group set up standards and keep them at camp.
Activities coordinator		Keep all people aware of pending activities and help with each one.
Games director		Direct all planned games at camp.
Hike director		Direct all hikes at camp.

Crafts director	Direct all crafts at camp.
Song leader	Lead the singing while at camp; take charge of choosing songs to sing.
Journalist	Record camp happenings; make a copy for all campers.
Photographer	Bring camera and film; take pictures; take charge of getting film developed.

CAMPSITE

Like building a home, planning an outdoor living area can be a creative and meaningful experience. Many of the considerations are parallel except that a campsite is temporary and that part of the planning of a campsite includes removing every trace of your stay. *Plan to meet your needs, but do not change the beauties of nature.* Good mottoes for an outdoorsman are these: "Leave an area better than you found it," and "Leave nothing but tracks and take nothing but pictures."

Selection of Campsite

To use out-of-the-way camping areas, whether they are public or private, it is important that you obtain permission from landowners or government agencies. Select a campsite using the following criteria:

Suitability

Are there places for a kitchen area, a fire area, toilet facilities, and an area for sleeping? Investigate the campsite ahead of time to assess its facilities, or at least arrive early enough to set up camp.

Protection

First consideration should be given to the safety of the campers. Place tents and camping equipment on high ground in the event of unexpected floods. Do not choose a spot directly in the path of prevailing canyon winds that might cause your camping or eating areas to fill with smoke. Use existing vegetative screenage to provide protection and privacy.

Conservation

Choose a site where camp activities will not harm the natural beauty of the land. Special precautions should be taken to assure that no one carves trees, picks wild flowers, or cuts green trees or branches. Follow already established trails. Do not destroy a natural habitat. Choose an area that will not permit sparks from the fire to spread or endanger vegetation.

Provisions

Is the site near water and dry wood? If it isn't, make special arrangements to bring them in.

The complexity of the camping area will depend upon your need and the length of your stay. The following suggestions offer some possibilities for different types of campsite areas.

Kitchen

In the outdoor kitchen, as indoors, everything will run more smoothly if there is a basic organization with specific areas for performing all duties. The kitchen might include cooking area, food storage areas for both refrigerated and staple foods, equipment area, food preparation and eating areas, and a cleanup area.

Cooking Area

An essential part of camping is planning and establishing the cooking area. Many established campsites have built-in fire areas which should be used. If you are camping in an area where no fire area is established, you will need to prepare one. Select from the following the type of fire area that will meet your needs.

Keyhole fire

An excellent plan that will serve for both the fire and the cooking area is the keyhole fire (figs. 10, 11). Build the fire in the circle area and draw hot coals (for cooking) from the fire into the square area, or lower part of the keyhole. For more cooking area make a double keyhole by forming a second square on the opposite side of the circle, or fire area. If desired, place a wire grill over the square (fig. 12).

Fig. 10. Preparing the keyhole fire

Fig. 11. The keyhole fire

Trench fire

A practical cooking area if digging is permitted is the trench. Dig a narrow trench approximately 1½ feet deep. Place wet logs or rocks on both sides of the trench level enough to support a pan with an end on each log, spanning the trench, or lay a wire rack over the trench. Build a fire in the trench or, if the trench is connected to a fire, draw the coals from the fire into the trench. The length of the trench will vary with the number of pans used (fig. 13).

Storage of Food
Staple foods

All food requires protection from small animals and insects. Wooden boxes with tight-fitting lids work well, as does either a box or a sack hung from a tree limb. If rodents are a problem, tie a knot in the rope and slip a can above the knot; this will prevent rodents from crawling down the rope into the stored food (fig. 14).

One of the best ways to organize a food supply for a group is to use a tent. Inside the tent everything should be placed in tight containers — plastic or cardboard — sturdy enough to keep rodents out. It can then be organized according to particular needs for each meal or by category, such as spices and seasonings, canned goods, and mixed ingredients. The organization should be clear enough that the cooks can easily find what they need.

Perishable foods

Select from the following four types of refrigerators the one that will best fit your needs.

Fig. 12. Wire grill over keyhole fire

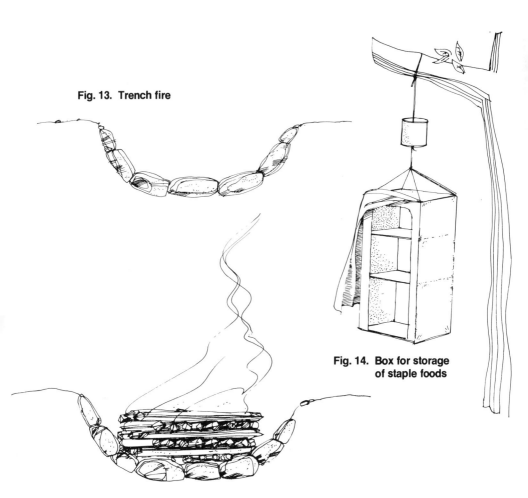

Fig. 13. Trench fire

Fig. 14. Box for storage of staple foods

Creek

The refrigerator may simply be a shady, shallow spot at the edge of the creek. Here perishables can be placed in the cool water in a burlap sack, a wooden crate, or another type of container. The container should be anchored by placing rocks in and around it or by tying it to a tree at the edge of the stream (fig. 15).

Ground

Dig a hole in a shady spot. The hole should be of sufficient size and depth to permit perishables to be placed below the surface of the ground. The top should be covered with burlap saturated with water. The burlap will remain wet by absorption if one end of the burlap is placed in a pan of water (fig. 16).

24

Fig. 15. Creek refrigerator

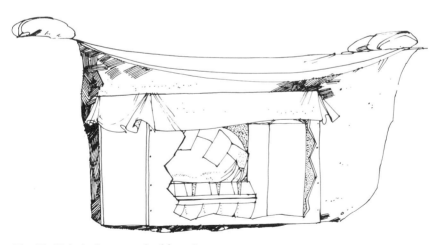

Fig. 16. Hole-in-the-ground refrigerator

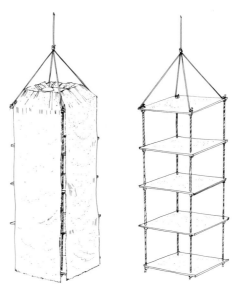

Fig. 17. Hanging portable burlap cooler

Burlap cooler

A hanging portable cooler can be made from burlap, ¼ - to ½ - inch plywood, and rope (fig. 17). Cut three or more squares of plywood into two-foot squares (or the size desired). Drill holes the size of a small rope in each corner, then thread the rope through the corner holes. Tie knots the distance desired between the shelves. Hang the shelves by the rope ends from a tree (in a cool, shady place) and cover them with burlap. The front should be overlapped so that the burlap can be separated for access. Extend the burlap above the top of the cooler sufficiently to be immersed in a pan of water. The burlap should be stapled or attached to all edges of the shelves except in the center front. If the burlap is saturated with water to begin with and the top of the burlap is kept in a pan of water, it will stay wet by absorption and will be an effective cooler because of evaporation.

Ice box

A commercial ice box in which either ice or dry ice is used is handy and effective. Items such as drinking water in milk cartons or juices, soft drinks, and other items in cans can be frozen and placed in the ice box. Do not freeze liquid in bottles; they will break. Milk may be frozen in order to help keep the box cool although the freezing process separates the protein and changes the flavor somewhat. If this happens, shake it well before drinking. Commercial ice or specially made products can also be purchased for coolers.

Storage Hints

For the storage of particular items, follow these suggestions:

- If cheese is to be stored for a long period of time, wrap it in cheesecloth dipped in vinegar. This will keep it from molding.
- Place a piece of apple, lemon, or orange inside a covered container of brown sugar to keep the sugar soft.
- Prevent salt from lumping by placing rice in the salt shaker. The rice will absorb the moisture and keep the salt dry.
- Place sugar, powdered sugar, and salt and pepper in large salt shakers with lids (fig. 18). Before traveling, unscrew the lids, place plastic wrap over the shaker, and screw the lid over the wrap. This prevents the sugar or salt from spilling. In camp, remove the wrap. Be sure the shakers are either labeled or color coded to indicate their contents.
- If bananas or avocados are green, store them in plastic bags. The gases given off by the fruit will speed ripening.
- Prepare ahead of time the necessary quantities of muffin and biscuit mix, blending all ingredients except liquid and eggs. Many other foods can be measured and prepackaged before leaving home.
- Store dry bread crumbs in plastic containers or plastic bags to use for augmenting meat and eggs. Use pastry crumbs or cake crumbs as toppings for puddings and desserts.
- To store eggs, break them into a quart jar or plastic container with a tight seal. They will pour out one at a time. If the plastic container has a spout, the eggs will come out of the spout one at a time. Use them within four days. Another way to store eggs is to roll them in pieces of newspaper and place them in a number-ten can, or pack them in flour, sugar, or sawdust. If you store them with the large end up, they will stay fresh longer. To check its freshness, place an egg in water. If it sits at the bottom of the pan, it is fresh. If it rises and floats in the water, moisture has been lost from the egg and it is not fresh.
- Place bread in a shoe box or plastic container to keep it from becoming smashed.
- Place items from glass jars in plastic containers so that they will not get broken in travel.
- Always buy butter or margarine in plastic containers so that it may be kept safely; then either burn or throw away the container.

Fig. 18. Powdered sugar in salt shaker

Fig. 19. Log bench

28

Food Preparation Area

Many campsites have tables available which can be used for preparing food. If a table is not available, spread a tarp on a flat rock or on the ground. Keep the area organized and clean as you work. Return all supplies to their storage area when they are no longer needed. Rinse all dishes used in preparing food before the food dries and becomes difficult to remove.

Eating Area

If a table is not available, select a shady spot and spread out a large piece of plastic or an army poncho. To add a special touch, prepare a centerpiece for the table. People often enjoy the warmth and informality of eating around the campfire. A large log can be used for seating, or a special log bench can be constructed, following these steps:

■ Saw two five- to eight-inch (in diameter) logs about two feet long.
■ Cut a groove in the top of each of these logs so that another log can rest in the grooves without rolling.
■ Place the small wedged logs on each end of the long log you will use as a seat (fig. 19).

Cleanup Area

The cleanup area is important for health and sanitation. Time can be saved if efficient cleanup procedures are followed. Special effort should be made to prevent unnecessary cleanup work.

Helpful Hints

■ Soap the outsides of all pans before using them on an open fire (fig. 20). Liquid detergent or lathered soap can be used. This will make it possible to wash the black off the pans more easily.
■ Line cooking equipment with foil to save on dishwashing (fig. 21).
■ Use paper towels to wipe dishes and to wipe the grease out of pans before washing them with water.
■ Put the dishwater on to heat before the meal begins. Gallon cans work very well for heating water.
■ Use salt or sand to clean off still-warm cast-iron grills.

Constant hot water

With a five-gallon square can and a long-necked funnel you can construct a hot-water tank. Poke a hole in the side of the can large enough to allow the neck of the funnel to go all the way into the

Fig. 20. Soaping outside of pans

Fig. 21. Pan lined with foil

Fig. 22. Hot water tank

can. The funnel should be placed in the exact spot shown in the diagram so that it will be far enough away from the spout yet away from the fire also (fig. 22). Place the can on its side, filled with water up to its original opening, and place the tank in the hot coals near the fire. When you need a cup of hot water, place an empty container under the spout. Pour a cup of cold water through the funnel. One cup of hot water will come out.

Washing dishes

There are several ways of doing dishes on a camping trip. Select the one which will best fit your needs and your environment. Soapy hot water will be important in getting dishes clean. If the water is not clean enough to drink, add a little liquid bleach to the dishwater or boil the rinse water and dip dishes into it to kill any germs.

Fig. 23. Double sink

A cloth or net bag may be made for an individual's eating dishes. A draw string should be pulled around the top so that dishes can be put into the bag, and the bag can be closed before it is dropped into boiling water to sterilize the contents. Afterwards, the bag may be tied to a rope which has been stretched between trees or to the limbs of a tree so that the dishes may dry.

Outdoor dishpans can be made by digging two holes near each other the desired depth, one for washing and one for rinsing the dishes. Line these holes with a ground cloth such as a poncho or a large piece of plastic. Each hole serves as a sink, and the lined edges serve as drainboards (fig. 23). Dishes can be wiped or placed in a bag to dry. A number-ten can will also serve well as a dishpan.

Storage of Equipment
Hanging Equipment Bag

A hanging purse bag with see-through sections is very effective as a storage place for equipment. Items can be categorized and placed in each see-through section. The sections can be stitched or partially stitched at one end to keep equipment from sliding out. Paper plates, napkins, and utensils for cooking and eating fit well in the bag. The vinyl covering keeps supplies and equipment dry when it rains (fig. 24).

Fig. 24. Hanging equipment bag

Equipment Rack

An equipment rack can be improvised from a man's traveling suit bag which zips in the front and is about four inches deep. Pockets designed to hold various types of equipment can be constructed. For example, a shoe bag or a section from a shoe bag sews easily into the back of the bag (fig. 25). Equipment can be transported easily and will remain organized and clean in this type of container.

Equipment Box

A wooden box can become a permanent equipment storage place. One side swings open from the top and becomes the front opening, held on each side by a chain so that it can be used also as a table. On each bottom corner of the box a molding is secured to hold the end of a pipe which becomes one of four legs to keep the box at working level. Holes are drilled in the sides near the top of the box to slide the pipes through when storing or carrying the box. The pipes should be longer than the width of the box so that they can be used as handles (fig. 26).

Garbage Area

Burning and removing are the two major ways to dispose of trash. The burnable material, which can simply go into the fire, should always be kept separate from the unburnable material. If

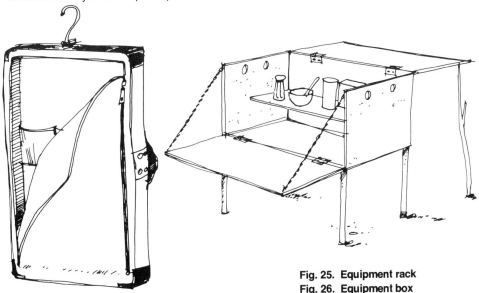

Fig. 25. Equipment rack
Fig. 26. Equipment box

trash barrels are provided at a campground, use them carefully, keeping all the trash picked up around the barrel.

If garbage must be carried from the campsite, burn as much as possible. Empty cans should have both ends removed, be flattened, and be placed in bags ready for removal. Fruit and vegetable peelings, cores, and rinds can be placed on newspaper and burned.

If it is permissible to dig in your camping area, dig a pit 2½ feet deep and one foot wide in which to pour grease. Fill the lower six inches of the pit with pebbles, placing large pebbles on the bottom, smaller pebbles next, and large pebbles on the top. Simply pour grease over the rocks in the pit. Be sure the pit is covered well at the final camp cleanup and that no trace of it exists when you leave camp.

Bring the garbage back with you from hikes. Do not leave it on the trails. Gum and candy wrappers litter the hillsides. They should be placed in pockets until they can be disposed of permanently with the trash.

Equipment Area

Every piece of camping equipment should have a special place for its storage — "A place for everything and everything in its place." There are some good general rules to follow in the use and storage of camping equipment:

- *Safety first.* There should be a chopping or sawing area where these pieces of equipment are to be used. Keep other people a safe distance away while you are cutting or sawing wood. Take precautions against the axe's slipping and cutting your leg or the saw's tearing your fingers. When you use a knife, always cut away from yourself. Be careful with equipment that contains kerosene or other liquid fuels; follow the directions on their labels.

- *Proper use.* Use the proper tool for the proper job. Don't abuse equipment by stabbing a knife into the ground or using the side of the axe to pound pegs.

- *Proper repair.* Repair broken equipment when you return from a trip before putting it away; then it will be ready to use when needed. Do not use partially broken equipment. You may damage it beyond repair. If you keep cutting equipment sharp and in good repair it will give you good service.

- *Proper storage.* Always place saws, axes, hatchets, and knives in their proper storage places when not in use. To prevent rust from forming on the metal parts of equipment, cover all cutting blades or metal parts with sheaths or wrap them in heavy canvas when not in use. Keep this equipment off the ground and well protected from moisture. Be careful not to store gas- or oil-filled equipment so that it will drip out. Clean all equipment before you store it.

Sleeping Area

For sleeping, choose a smooth, flat area, free from bumps, roots, and immovable rocks. If the area seems too flat and hard, it can be helpful to dig out a "hip hole" before laying down your bedding (fig. 27). Always choose a spot where you are protected from the elements. The sleeping area could be sheltered by the natural surroundings (trees, bushes), or coverings could be made with plastic or ponchos.

Do not choose an area that will collect drainage from rains or a swampy or moist area where there are numerous mosquitoes. Be careful to keep away from dead, overhanging branches, dead and rotten trees, or dangerous, loose rocks on hillsides or rock walls.

Fig. 27. "Hip hole" for sleeping area

Fig. 28. Water spout

Bathroom Area
Washing and Cleaning Up

Take a large plastic bleach bottle and poke a pinhole in the front near the bottom to make a spout. Fill the bottle with water. When you are ready to wash your hands, loosen the lid; the pressure from the top will force a small stream of water from the spout. When the lid is airtight (a plastic lining will keep a leaky lid airtight) the water will stay inside the jug. If the hole grows larger, plug it with a toothpick. To use a larger stream of water from the jug, poke the hole with a golf tee, tie the tee to the jug handle, and use the tee as a stopper.

Attach a rope to the handle and tie the jug onto a tree limb. Place a bar of soap in a nylon stocking or a piece of net and tie it to the handle, or a small hole may be drilled through the center of the soap and the soap attached to the handle with heavy string. Add interest to the jug by painting a face on it with the mouth over the spout area, or add decals for decoration (fig. 28).

Shower or Bath

Use a variation of the bleach bottle for a shower. Punch holes in the bottom of a bottle and hang it high in the tree. Stop the holes with golf tees; tie each golf tee to a string hooked to the handle of the bottle so that they will not get lost. Control the force of water by pulling out the desired number of golf tees.

A spray bottle can also be used for a shower. For privacy, construct a curtain for the shower out of ponchos or plastic.

A bathtub can be improvised by digging a hole in the ground the desired size and shape. Line the hole with a large piece of plastic and fill it with water.

If it is not possible to dig a hole in the ground, drape the heavy plastic over four logs which have been placed in a rectangular shape (fig. 29).

Toilet

It is best to use available facilities if they exist, but there is wisdom in knowing how to construct a latrine or a portable toilet.

A deep hole or straddle trench should always be dug for a latrine — in a private spot and at least 100 feet away from any source of water. If the toilet is conveniently flanked by two trees, poles lashed to the trees will furnish a good place to sit. Place the roll of toilet paper on the shovel handle or on the end of a stick

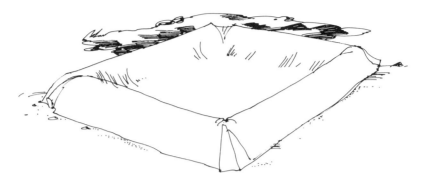

Fig. 29. Plastic bathtub

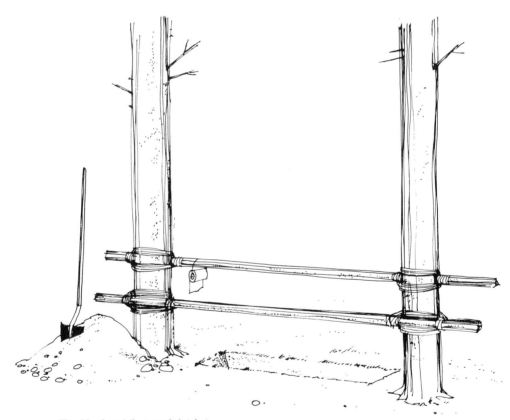

Fig. 30. Straddle-trench latrine

lashed to a tree (fig. 30).

A portable toilet can be purchased from a camping goods store or constructed from a wooden crate lined with plastic garbage bags.

Always keep a shovel handy to cover body waste with dirt or ashes to keep flies away.

Leaving a Campsite

All of us like to arrive at a clean campsite. It is only good manners to leave it clean for the next campers. Some good tips to remember in caring for a campsite before you leave are as follows:

Trash Area

Always use designated cans if they are available. Burn as much garbage as you can, and if garbage cans are not provided, take the rest with you when you leave. Fill with dirt any holes you have dug.

Fire and Cooking Area

Use only designated fire areas or the areas you build. When you are ready to leave, if you are in an undeveloped area, bury the ashes or take them with you. If you have built your own fire area, restore it to its natural state. All fireplace rocks and other stones should be removed. Any sticks or wires used in cooking should be taken care of properly. If a pit was dug, all partially burned coals need to be buried in the hole and covered well with dirt.

Storage Areas

Any shelves or poles lashed to trees should be removed. Burn all lashing twine or carry it out with you.

Bathroom Area

Latrine holes should be buried carefully. Lashed seats should be removed.

In general, all areas you were using while camping should be returned to their natural state. Again, leave a campsite in better condition than you found it.

Fig. 31. Safe fire area

Fig. 32. Tinder, kindling, and fuel

40

FIREBUILDING

Fire building is an essential skill in outdoor cooking. Prepare to master fire building before learning to cook. A basic need for a camp is a good fire not only for cooking but for warmth and for protection from animals at night. Improperly made or tended fires can become destructive. Take precautions in preparing fires and putting them out by following a few simple rules.

Rules To Follow

Be sure to follow the fire rules of the particular area you are visiting.

- For building the fire, select a spot fifteen feet from trees, bushes, and fallen trees. Fires built over roots are dangerous because the fire can follow the roots back to the trees or bushes and cause larger fires. Never build the fire directly under branches or near dry grass or weeds. When possible, either use rocks to enclose the area where you plan to build the fire or dig a fire pit or trench and clear away flammable fuel within a ten-foot area around the fire (fig. 31).
- Build the fire only large enough to satisfy your needs. Big fires are not required in cooking; too much heat makes it difficult to control the cooking temperature. Most cooking can be done best on hot coals rather than on direct flames.
- Never leave a fire unattended, and always have a bucket of water and a shovel near the fire to extinguish it in case of emergency. Report any wild fire to the nearest forest or fire officer as soon as possible. Put out your fire and your matches — dead out.
- Before leaving the campsite, make sure the fuel is cool, the fire is completely out, the ashes are buried (if you are in a primitive area), and the fireplace area is back to its natural state.

Woodpile

Upon your arrival at the campsite, your first and perhaps most important activity is building a good-sized woodpile. After you are in the process of cooking, it is inconvenient to stop and look for wood. Outdoor meals are more successful if an ample supply of wood is available during the cooking time.

Piling the wood

Care in piling wood can protect it from moisture. Begin at least ten or fifteen feet from the fire circle. Place side by side horizontally two large poles, on which to place the wood so that it will be protected from ground dampness. Stack the wood into separate stacks: tinder, kindling, and fuel, placing the stack of fuel closest to the fire, since it is used most often (fig. 32). Large sticks can be driven into the ground to divide the stacks. Use a large piece of plastic or a poncho to cover the woodpile when it rains.

Types of wood

The three basic types of wood to gather are tinder, kindling, and fuel.

■ *Tinder.*   For material to start the fire, use anything that will burn which is smaller than your little finger. Some examples of tinder are dry grass, dry leaves, small twigs, dry pine needles from evergreen trees, fine shavings, and bark.

A fuzz stick, carved from a small twig, will catch fire more rapidly than another twig (fig. 33). After a rain the best place to find dry wood is on the lower inside branches of little evergreen trees.

Good tinder can be prepared at home in egg cartons. Fill each egg cup with dry, red pine needles, pieces of paper, and any other dry materials that will burn quickly. Pour paraffin over the material. Then place a looped string in the wax to be used later as a wick (fig. 34). When it becomes difficult to start a fire because of wet wood or other reasons, cut one of the egg cups off and place the other tinder around it (fig. 35). After the carton is lighted, it will create a large flame which should burn for about ten minutes.

Cotton balls soaked in paraffin or bottle caps filled with paraffin and topped off with a string wick also make good fire-starting materials.

■ *Kindling.* Kindling is wood which ranges in diameter from the size of the little finger to the size of the wrist. It is used to feed the fire until larger pieces of wood will burn.

■ *Fuel.* Pieces of wood the size of the wrist and larger are classed as fuel. This type of wood is used to sustain the fire.

Fig. 33. Fuzz stick as tinder

Fig. 34. Tinder prepared in egg carton

Fig. 35. Egg-cup tinder

Fig. 36. Basic A-frame with teepee kindling

Building an A-Frame

- Make a basic A-frame, or triangle, in the center of the fire-circle with three sticks approximately one inch in diameter and one-half foot long. One end of each stick should overlap another stick, and the other end should rest on the ground.
- In the center of the A-frame make a teepee with tinder, starting with very fine materials and graduating to more coarse materials. Place some kindling around the teepee (fig. 36).
- Over the A-frame lay the type of fire structure you desire. Light the tinder while it is still accessible, even if the fire structure is not entirely laid.
- Lay the fire structure so that air can circulate between the materials. Without enough air the fire will not continue to burn. If necessary, fan the smoldering fire with a paper plate to aid the circulation of air.

Types of Fires

Fires are generally named from the manner in which the wood is stacked.

Teepee

A basic fire used to begin other fires is the teepee fire. Lay the A-frame and the tinder. Then set the kindling and fuel on end in the form of a teepee (fig. 37). The high flames of this fire are good for one-pot cooking and for the reflector oven.

Log cabin fire

To get a good bed of coals, build the log cabin fire by forming a basic A-frame and a teepee of tinder, then placing logs in the center as if you were building a miniature log cabin. Gradually lay the logs toward the center as you build the cabin. It will have the appearance of a pyramid, and coals will form quickly (fig. 38).

Crisscross fire

For a large, deep bed of coals for Dutch oven cooking or roasting, prepare a crisscross fire. After forming a basic A-frame and a teepee of tinder and kindling, place the logs on the fire in layers, one layer crossing the other. Leave a little space between each log for air to circulate (fig. 39).

Indian or star fire

This fire is sometimes called the lazy man's fire because, as the logs burn down, they are simply pushed farther into the flames

Fig. 37. Teepee fire

Fig. 38. Log cabin fire

Fig. 39. Crisscross fire

Fig. 40. Indian or star fire

(fig. 40). It is a useful fire for preparing one-pot meals. Use the basic A-frame and the teepee of tinder and kindling to begin the fire, then feed the long logs into the center as needed.

Methods of Starting a Fire

There are many ways to achieve actual combustion. Some of the more primitive methods need be used only in times of emergency.

Matches

The most common method of starting a fire is to use matches. They can be protected against moisture by dipping them into either paraffin wax or fingernail polish. After dipping them in wax, place them in the holes of corrugated cardboard, then roll the cardboard (fig. 41). It should be transported in a waterproof container.

Flashlight batteries and steel wool

A rather dramatic method of starting a fire is to conduct the electricity from two flashlight batteries through steel wool: Use 00 or a finer grade steel-wool roll, cut or tear it into a ½-inch strip (which will lengthen out to a strip seven or eight inches long), and use two flashlight batteries; old batteries will work as well as new ones. As shown in the illustration, place one battery on top of the other making sure both are in an upright position. Take one end of the strip of steel wool and hold it against the bottom of the lower battery. Then take the other end of the wool and rub it across the top of the top battery. After the steel wool sparks, place it next to the tinder and blow on it to start the fire (figs. 42-44).

Fig. 41. Matches dipped in paraffin

46

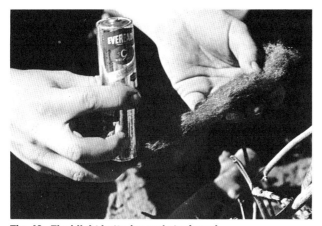
Fig. 42. Flashlight batteries and steel wool

Fig. 43. Steel wool brushing top battery

Fig. 44. Blowing on the ignited steel wool

Flint and steel

A meat-cutter's steel, a steel knife blade, or a file struck against stone will cause sparks. The sparks will create a thin wisp of smoke if they come in contact with very dry tinder. When smoke appears, blow gently with short puffs of air until the tinder bursts into flame. Very fine tinder or charred cloth will facilitate ignition.

Magnifying glass

A strong magnifying glass placed in the direct sunlight so that a fine point of light is focused into dry tinder will cause the tinder to smoke and eventually break into flame.

Bow drill

If constructed properly, a bow drill, consisting of a fireboard, a drill, a socket, and a bow, will create heat that can light tinder. A notch must be cut in the side of a fireboard through which a drill will pass and rest on a flat grooved surface below (fig. 45). A socket (lubricated with grease) to fit the hand will allow the drill, operated with the string of a bow, to rotate first one way and then another until a fine, hot dust results (fig. 46). The dust will smoke when it becomes heated. Then it should be placed into the tinder and blown into flame (fig. 47).

Extinguishing a Fire

Knowing how to extinguish a fire properly is as important as, if not more important than, knowing how to start one. First, break up the fire with a stick and spread out the coals. Sprinkle water over the coals. Keep stirring the fire with the stick and drenching it with water until the coals are cool enough to touch. Take precautions not to pour large quantities of water on a hot fire because a sudden issue of steam might burn bystanders. A fire is not out until the coals are cool enough to touch. If large logs have been burning, make sure all sparks are put out.

If no water is available, dig a hole or a trench and bury all hot material, or stir dirt thoroughly through the hot material and cover it with dirt at least two inches deep.

Heat When Open Fires Are Not Permitted

In many camping areas open fires are illegal because of fire hazard. Increasingly, picnickers are forced to use other methods of heat for cooking food out of doors.

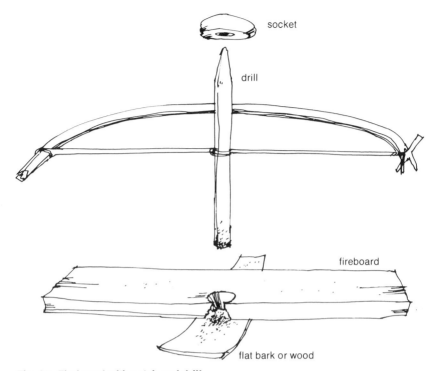

socket

drill

fireboard

flat bark or wood

Fig. 45. Fireboard with notch and drill

Fig. 46. Hot dust **Fig. 47. Hot dust in tinder**

Above photos courtesy of Larry Dean Olsen's *Outdoor Survival Skills*, Brigham Young University Press

Tablets

Commercial tablets, available at camping-goods stores, can be placed in a small stove and lighted. These tablets are about one inch in diameter and about ½-inch thick. They are very good for warming canned food and for cooking things that don't take long periods of time. They may be used either with the tin-can stove or with a small commercial stove made expressly for their use. If a stove is not available, place stones in close proximity around the tablets to serve as a stand to hold small cooking pots and cans (figs. 48, 49).

Canned heat

Canned heat can be commercially purchased and used for cooking or warming food in cans. Special stoves made to use with canned heat may be purchased (fig. 50).

Fig. 48. Commercial tablets

Fig. 49. Heating pork and beans

Paraffin

Make your own can of heat by rolling narrow strips of corrugated cardboard into a tuna-fish can and filling the can with paraffin. Step-by-step directions are in the section on the tin-can stove.

Newspapers

Newspapers can be used in the tall-can stove for cooking meat as shown in the section on the tall-can stove.

Charcoal briquets

Charcoal is one of the best kinds of fuel to use when open fires are not permitted or when it is against the law for wood to be gathered. Charcoal briquets are good for grilling meat, for cooking foil meals, for spit or stick cooking, and for the Dutch oven. Charcoal briquets should never be burned in a closed area. They give off carbon monoxide which can be deadly. Two rules to

Fig. 50. Canned heat

remember when you are using charcoal briquets are these: (1) never light the briquets with homemade lighting fluid or gasoline; it could explode. Also, the briquets tend to give food an offensive flavor. (2) Always allow forty to fifty minutes for the briquets to become hot.

A good way to shorten the preparation time of charcoal briquets and to insure an even heat is to use the chimney starter method. Using two or three sheets of newspaper, matches, and a number-ten tin can, follow these steps:

- Cut both ends out of the can.
- Punch holes every two inches around the lower edge of the can with a punch-type can opener.
- Set the can down so that the holes are next to the ground.
- Crumple two or three sheets of newspaper and place them in the bottom of the can.
- Place charcoal briquets on top of the crumpled newspaper.
- Lift the can and light the newspaper. Prop a bottom edge of the can on a rock to create a good draft. The briquets will be ready to use in thirty to forty minutes (fig. 51).
- If a greater draft is necessary, prop the can on small rocks and fan the flames with a paper plate.
- When the briquets are hot, lift the chimney off the coals and spread the coals out. They are ready to use.

The chimney starter is also useful for more rapid heating of briquets when lighter fluid is used. The can will insure an even heat for all the fuel.

Egg carton briquet starters: Another way of lighting the briquets is to use wax in a cardboard egg carton. Separate the lid from an egg carton and set the bottom of the carton inside the lid. A little wax poured inside the lid first will make the cupped half adhere to it. Then pour approximately ¼ inch of melted paraffin into each egg cup and let the wax cool. When it is cool, set a charcoal briquet in each cup, then continue to stack briquets over the carton. Light the carton and wait for the briquets to heat (fig. 52).

Starting briquets over a campfire: Briquets can also be added to wood fires to provide a better and larger bed of coals. Pour the briquets into the hot fire and allow them to heat for twenty to thirty minutes. An effective way to start charcoal briquets over an open fire is to shape a screen (½- to ¾-inch mesh) into a bucket or bowl-shaped basket. Make a wire bale for lifting or carrying. Place the desired amount of charcoal briquets into the basket and set it over an open fire (fig. 53). If the fire is hot, particularly if there are good flames, the charcoal will start quickly, and it will all heat evenly.

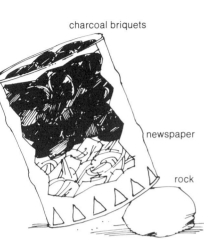

charcoal briquets

newspaper

rock

Fig. 51. Chimney starter

Fig. 52. Egg carton briquet

Fig. 53. Portable basket of hot briquets

Commercial starters: Commercially prepared charcoal starters and jellies can be purchased. It is important that you put the right amount of the mixture on the briquets, close the container of the starter, and place it out of the way of sparks or flames before lighting the briquets.

Electric starters: If electricity is available, it can be used to start the briquets. Place an electric coil in the fire bed and place the briquets over these.

Extinguishing briquets: Use your briquets over and over again until they are burned out. Put them out by using one of the following methods: 1) Place them in a can which can be covered with a lid or with foil. The cover cuts off the oxygen supply, and the briquets will cease to burn. 2) Place them in a can of water. The briquets must be allowed to dry before using them again.

METHODS OF COOKING

Preparing foods out-of-doors is especially satisfying because there are some ways of cooking which cannot be duplicated in an indoor kitchen. Moreover, out-of-doors preparation adds the extra ingredients of woodsmoke flavoring and fresh-air, lacking in the home kitchen. With a keen outdoor appetite, cool mountain mornings, and a good warm fire, a camper is ready for a nutritious outdoor breakfast, is anxious to pack a hiking lunch, and is even willing to dig a pit for an evening meal.

The following carefully tested methods of preparing foods will add interest and variety to your whole camping experience. This chapter is designed to give you ideas on how familiar indoor cooking methods and principles can be duplicated in the outdoor kitchen setting. Refer to the following chart for outdoor methods which can be used to accomplish familiar desired results. Then look for instructions in the following pages for a particular method of outdoor cooking to see what type of fire to build; the equipment you will need to gather, purchase, or make; suggestions on foods to use; and step-by-step directions to follow. With the variety of easy ways of preparing foods available to you, camp cooking should never become dull or routine. A feeling of pride and satisfaction will accompany a well-prepared meal in the out-of-doors.

Indoor Cooking Method Duplicated in Outdoor Setting

Bake: Cook with dry heat
Tin can stove
Dutch oven
Can oven
Reflector oven
Pit cooking
Food inside of food
Sand cooking

Barbecue: Cook over direct heat and season with seasoned sauce
Stick and spit
Can barbecue
Tall can

Boil: Cook in water
Aluminum foil
Tin can, billy can
Dutch oven
Liquid in paper cup or sack
Double boiler

Braise: Sauté in a small amount of fat, then cook slowly in covered pan with liquid
Aluminum foil
Tin can stove
Dutch oven
Pit cooking

Broil: Cook by direct heat
Can barbecue
Reflector oven
Cooking directly on coals

Fry: Cooking with small amount of fat
Aluminum foil
Tin can stove
Dutch oven
Rock cooking

Roast: Cook with dry heat
Tin can stove
Dutch oven
Can oven
Reflector oven
Pit cooking

Steam: Cook with moist heat
Aluminum foil
Dutch oven

Stew: Cooking for a long time in small amount of liquid
Dutch oven
Pit cooking

Stick and Spit Cooking

Probably the most commonly used method of outdoor food preparation is stick cooking, which can be an exciting way to involve each camper in the preparation of his own meal. This method is most often used to prepare meats and breads. The combination of meat, fruits, and vegetables prepared on a stick is commonly called the shish kebab (fig. 54).

Spit cooking is very similar to stick cooking. The main difference is in the amount of food to be cooked. Larger amounts of food can be cooked on a spit.

Principle

Much like using a broiler or a rotisserie at home where dry heat is used, food is placed on a stick, held near the coals, and rotated until cooked.

Fire(s)

Always use hot coals to cook foods on a stick rather than direct flames. Good coals can be made from a crisscross fire or a log cabin fire (see chapter on firebuilding). Charcoal briquets can also be used if coals are needed for a longer period of time.

For a spit, a large fire is good because you can have the needed amount of coals available all the time.

Equipment Needs
Stick cooking

Either a stick, a wood dowel, or wire coat hanger is needed for stick cooking. Cut a straight green stick about ½ inch in diameter and four feet long; sharpen to a point on one end. Willows, usually growing near stream beds, work well.

Adapt a coat hanger for stick cooking by untwisting the hanger at the top and unfolding it until it is straight. To make a handle, place three empty thread spools on one end and bend the wire extending behind them around to the front of the spools and turn the end around the wire to secure them onto the hanger. A shorter-handled stick can be made by simply straightening the hook of a coat hanger for a place to put the food and pulling out the center of the bottom of the hanger to straighten it into a double-wire handle. This will make a stronger handle (fig. 55).

Spit cooking

Stick. Use a stick about ½ inch in diameter and one to two feet longer than the fireplace area. A small stick can be lashed onto

Fig. 54. Stick cooking: the shish kebab

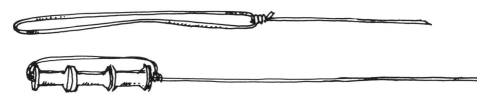

Fig. 55. Coat hanger for stick cooking

Fig. 56. Spit cooking

this stick to make it easier to turn. It is a good idea not to strip the bark from the stick because food will slip more easily on a slick surface. Just wash the bark with soap and rinse it. Cut and pound into the ground on either side of the fireplace area two forked sticks tall enough to hold the spit about two feet above the hot coals (fig. 56). If there are flat rocks in the area, pile two stacks to take the place of the two forked sticks (fig. 57). Bricks can also be stacked. To keep the stick from rolling off the bricks, place one stick in each of the two brick holes on both sides. The spit will fit between the sticks to hold it securely (fig. 58).

Pipe. If you are using a pipe, determine the length of it by the amount of food you plan to cook on the spit. Drill two or three holes in the center of the pipe for threading wire or heavy string through to anchor the food to the pipe. A metal spit may have a handle welded on one end to make it easier to turn.

Use sturdy, green, forked sticks to hold the pipe, or prepare two pipes by welding three U-shaped pieces of half pipe to the sides of two 3-foot pieces of pipe. The three pipes will serve as brackets, making it possible to change the height of the spit (fig. 59). Stacked rocks or bricks work well, also.

Care

Wooden sticks need to be burned or stacked neatly for other campers before you leave the camp site. Coat hangers may be cleaned easily either by placing the end of the wire in the hot coals to burn off the food or by using steel wool. If cleaned well after each use, this type of stick may be used over and over again. The metal spit equipment should be burned clean and wiped off for future use. Anything that is not kept should be properly disposed of.

Steps
Stick Cooking

- Place food(s) to be cooked on the stick or wire hanger. Hangers are good to use with shish kebabs because the food will slide easily onto the hangers. However, cut the food in small pieces so that they are not too heavy. Meats should be cut into thin strips and double threaded onto the wire. Heavy foods will not turn around with the hanger.
- Place shish kebabs over the coals but not too near, or the food will be cooked on the outside and raw in the middle. If the food will take a long time to cook, find a rock to place under the stick

Fig. 57. Rocks supporting a wooden spit

Fig. 58. Brick support

Fig. 59. Pipes used to make a spit

near the handle and another to hold the stick down. Turn the stick periodically until the food is done.

■ If one item will take more time to cook than the others it can be partially precooked. A good example of this would be the meat used for shish kebabs. The meat can be boiled or fried first.

Spit cooking

Prepare the food to be placed on the spit by washing it, centering it on the pole, and basting it with sauce. If the food needs to be wired to the pipe (or the pole), begin at one end and wire one item at a time, making sure to put the wire or string through the holes if you are using a pipe. Be sure to wire the legs and wings of a chicken tightly to its body so they will not burn. (See fig. 58.)

Place the food over the coals and wait about five minutes to see if it is cooking properly. If it is cooking too fast, raise the spit; if too slow, lower it. Keep it slowly rotating. Food which takes a long period of time to cook, such as chicken, can be rotated at intervals of three to five minutes.

Tin Can Stove

The tin can stove is not only one of the most pleasure-giving and innovative outdoor cooking methods but is also an excellent item to have in the home for emergencies.

Principle

Heat is conducted to the top of a specially prepared gallon can where it can be used for frying, boiling, or baking. The tin can stove is best used to prepare food for only one or two people because of the limited amount of space (fig. 60).

Fire(s)

The two sources of heat that may be used for the tin can stove are (1) a wood fire built under the can, and (2) a buddy burner: a tuna can (or a can similar in shape) filled with rolled corrugated cardboard filled with paraffin wax.

Equipment Needs
Buddy burner

A tuna can, rolled corrugated cardboard, and paraffin wax.

Stove

A number-ten can (one gallon), tin snips, and a punch-type can opener.

Damper

Aluminum foil or tuna-can lid, wire, small nail, hammer, and coat hanger.

Oven

Three small flat rocks of equal size (approximately one-half inch high), a tuna can or its lid, a three-lb. shortening can (or a can of comparable size), and 1½ to 2 feet of pliable wire. If an oven with a window is desired, turkey oven wrap and wire will be needed. A tuna can or lid is used to hold the cooking food.

Preparation
Buddy burner

To make the burner, cut corrugated cardboard (across the corrugation so that its holes show) into strips which are the same width as the height of the tuna can. Roll the cardboard and place it in the can, then pour the melted wax over the cardboard (figs. 61, 62). Heat the wax in a double boiler because it if is overheated, it will burst into flames.

Fig. 60. Tin can stove

Fig. 61. Rolled cardboard

Fig. 62. Wax in buddy burner

Fig. 63. Lighting the wick

Fig. 64. Wax over buddy burner

Fig. 65. Smoke holes in tin can stove

Fig. 66. Foil damper

Fig. 67. Can lid damper

The cardboard in the buddy burner serves as a wick, and the wax serves as a candle to provide the heat for the stove. A small wick can be placed in the corrugated cardboard for fast and easy lighting. It is also helpful to turn the can on its side so that the flame can spread across the cardboard more easily (fig. 63). Filled with wax, it will burn for 1½ to 2 hours. To lengthen the time of the buddy burner's use, place a chunk of wax on top of the corrugation while it is burning. The burner can be used for an indefinite period of time if it is replenished with wax because the wax burns at a lower temperature than the cardboard, lengthening the life of the cardboard (fig. 64).

Stove

First, cut out one end of the number-ten can. Then cut a door about three inches high and four inches wide on a side of the can at the open end, leaving the top of the door attached. Pull the door open. Slide the cut-out lid into the can, settling it firmly against the closed end. The following procedure will hold it there permanently, and the double thickness of metal will conduct the heat more efficiently. At the top of the stove (the closed end of the can) punch four or five smoke holes around the side (fig. 65). The metal from the holes will hold the extra lid in place. Your stove is now complete. You will cook on the top of the can, or you may cover it with heavy-duty aluminum foil if it is available.

Damper

It is necessary to have a cover damper to control the heat on the buddy burner. These can be made out of foil or the lid of a can.

Foil. Fold a length of foil about 1½ times the diameter of the buddy burner. Obtain three or four thicknesses of the foil. Fold one end back a little more than the diameter of the can. This end is then placed on the can and adjusted back and forth to control the heat. The other end of the foil is bent at a 90-degree angle toward the ground to the height of the buddy burner. This end supports the damper and is used in adjusting it (fig. 66).

Lid. Make a damper from the lid of a can. The lid should be slightly smaller than the diameter of the buddy burner so that it will snuff out the flames in the center and permit the edges to burn. Now make a wire handle and attach it to the lid. This may be done with a coat hanger, preferably one that has a rolled cardboard around the bottom wire. Remove the cardboard and separate the wire where it is attached in the center. Bend the two sides together.

Make holes in the end of the lid and wire the two ends of the hanger to it. Bend the end of the handle at a 90-degree angle so that it forms a support to hold the end of the can flat to the buddy burner. The damper can be pulled forward and backward to control the heat (fig. 67).

Oven

Cut both ends out of a shortening can and wire see-through oven wrap tightly over one end so that the food is visible. Make a handle by hooking the end of a wire on each side of the can.

If a shortening can is not available, shape aluminum foil into a dome that will fit over the stove in the same manner. Foods will be placed in a tuna can or on its lid, will be set on the stove, and will have the shortening can or the foil dome placed over them to bake (fig. 68).

Foods

Foods which can be fried can be cooked on top of the can. Eggs in a basket, bacon, hamburgers, and tacos are a few of the foods which can be prepared on the tin can stove as a frying pan. When the stove is made into an oven, it can be used to bake cakes, pies, breads, vegetables, and some meats.

Steps

Frying

- Light the buddy burner and place it under the can.
- Place the damper over the buddy burner to create only the desired amount of heat. The can stove will be ready to be used in seconds (fig. 69).

Boiling

- Place food to be boiled in a can on the stove top.
- Light the burner and slide it under the stove. The liquid will soon be boiling.

Baking

- Place food on a tuna lid or, if it is cake batter or some other near-liquid, pour it into the clean, greased tuna can. Before doing this, however, if you think the food might stick to the tuna can, insert a folded one-inch strip of aluminum foil, folding it over the edge and down across the inside of the can, leaving enough foil over both edges to pull upward after the food has been cooked. The food should then remove easily.

Fig. 68. Can oven

Fig. 69. Can stove with buddy burner

67

- Place three rocks ½ inch high in a triangular shape on the stove-can.
- Place the tuna lid or can of batter on the rocks, which will not hold the food off the stove but will prevent the bottom from burning by allowing the air to circulate around the oven, which bakes the food.
- Cover the food with the shortening can and let it bake (fig. 70).

A good item to bake in the tin-can-stove oven is a pineapple upside-down cake. Grease the inside of the tuna can, then place the one-inch strip of aluminum foil in the can. Place one slice of pineapple in the can with a maraschino cherry in its center. Sprinkle one tablespoon of brown sugar over the pineapple and pour about one tablespoon of pineapple juice over that. Fill the can about two-thirds full of cake batter, then place it in the oven of the tin can stove. It will take about 20 minutes for the cake to brown (fig. 71).

Fig. 70. See-through oven

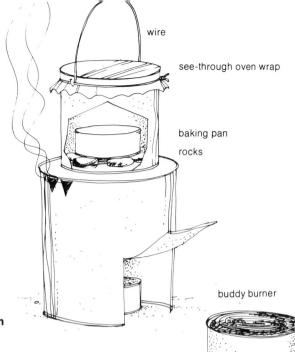

wire

see-through oven wrap

baking pan

rocks

buddy burner

**Fig. 71. Buddy burner in
tin-can-stove oven**

Aluminum Foil Cookery

Cooking in aluminum foil is the modern version of cooking food in leaves and clay. It is clean and easy, and there are no pots to carry or dishes to wash.

Principle

Aluminum foil is used to broil, braise, fry, sauté, and steam foods. Steaming, the most common method, is done by sealing the food in foil so that moisture cannot escape.

Fire(s)

A fire which will rapidly produce a two-inch bed of coals is necessary for foil cooking. A crisscross or log-cabin fire is best, but charcoal briquets are also good. When wood is at a premium or so soft that it burns too fast, use a combination of wood and briquets. (See the chapter on fire building.)

Equipment Needs

The basic equipment is aluminum foil, which can be purchased in regular and heavy-duty weights. The heavy-duty weight is more desirable because of its additional strength.

Preparation

To make a foil pan, cut a green willow switch flexible enough to make a loop at the end about the size of a frying pan. Secure the loop to the stock with wire or by tying it (fig. 72). If a loop cannot be made, cut a forked stick; cut off the forked ends evenly about four to eight inches beyond the forked joint, depending upon the size of pan desired. Whether you use the loop or the fork, cut a piece of foil which extends three inches beyond the size of the loop or the fork. If you desire the pan to have depth, allow the foil to sag in the middle. After forming the pan, roll the excess foil as far under and around the stick as possible (figs. 73, 74).

A frying pan can also be made from a coat hanger by straightening the hook and pulling the center bottom wire to form a square. Place foil across the wire and wrap it around twice. To make a handle, tightly wire the straightened hook to a stick so that it will not turn.

Foods

Foods such as meats, vegetables, and fruits are those most commonly cooked with foil, and steaming is the most common method used. Entire dinners are often put together and cooked in one piece of foil.

Foil cooking can be useful in many other ways:
- Warming bread.
- Cooking vegetables (corn on the cob, etc.).
- Frying bacon and eggs.
- Boiling small amounts of water or other liquids.

Steps

- Cut two pieces of light-weight foil or one piece of heavy-duty foil twice the circumference of the item to be wrapped.
- Place the food in the middle of the shiny side of one piece of foil. (Tests have proven that the shiny side of the foil reflects more radiant heat.)
- Add a little water if there is not much moisture in the food.
- Bring the opposite sides of the foil together and fold their ends over together ½ inch at a time, turning them down in small folds until they can be folded no longer.
- Flatten the top of the package and roll each open edge toward the center in small folds. The edges of the package must be tightly sealed. This is called the drugstore wrap.
- If the package needs to be wrapped again, place the folded top of the package downward in the center of the other piece of foil.

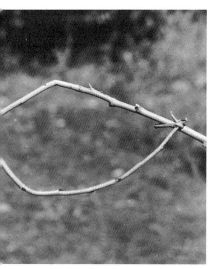

Fig. 72. Foil frying pan

Fig. 73. Fish in frying pan

Fig. 74. Hamburger in frying pan

Fig. 75. Food in foil

Fig. 76. Folding ends of foil

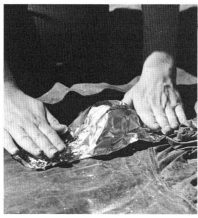

Fig. 77. Flattening the folded foil

Fig. 78. Rolling ends of foil

Fig. 79. Insulating food in newspaper

Wrap the second piece of foil exactly like the first, but if heavy-duty foil is used, one layer is usually enough (figs. 75-78).

If the coals are very hot or if you are using briquets, you can prevent the food from overcooking by rolling the first package of foil in three layers of newspaper before wrapping it in the second layer of foil (fig. 79). Another way to prevent overcooking is to place a vegetable which has a high moisture content around the food. For example: place sliced onions on both sides of a hamburger dinner; wrap a meat loaf in cabbage leaves; place tomato slices in a foil dinner. A third way to make sure your dinner does not burn is to turn the dinner every five minutes while it is on the coals to prevent one spot from getting too hot.

Tall Can Stove

The tall can stove is a quick method for cooking meats which have only a small amount of fat.

Principle

Dry heat given off from flaming newspapers cooks the meat on the rack in the stove. Juice from the meat drips down on the papers and keeps them burning. This method is much like barbecuing meats. Foods cooked in this manner will have a definite smoky flavor.

Fire(s)

The fuel for this method of cooking is rolled-up newspapers. Four or five sheets of newspapers are loosely twisted and crushed lightly into small "logs," then placed in the stove bottom. A single sheet of newspaper wadded and set on top of the logs is lighted first. The fats dripping from the meat will keep the log papers burning.

Do not use sections with colored ink that produce toxic fumes when burned.

Equipment Needs

Items needed to make a tall can stove: square five-gallon can and can opener, wire rack that fits on the can, newspapers, and water spray bottle or water pistol. Do not use refrigerator racks; they will give off toxic fumes, and they may melt in the heat.

Preparation

To build the stove, remove the top from a large can, such as a five-gallon honey can. You may need a knife and a hammer to cut around the corners. Cut a 2½-inch vent on opposite sides of the can about three inches from the bottom. Place a cookie cooling rack over the top of the can for the grill.

Foods

Meat which is not more than an inch thick and has some fat can be cooked on this stove.

Steps

- After the bottom of the can is filled with twisted rolls of newspaper, wad or crumple lightly about a half sheet of single newspaper and place it on the top of the rolled paper (fig. 80).
- When the stove is ready for cooking, set a match to the single sheet.
- Place the rack of meat on the stove.
- If the flames become too high, spray them with water from a spray bottle or a water pistol.
- If not enough fat drips from the meat to keep the flames burning, place two-inch strips of bacon or fat between the meat until the flames flare up (fig. 81).

Fig. 80. Newspaper crumpled in tall can stove

Fig. 81. Steak on tall can stove

74

Can Barbecue

The can barbecue is a simple method of preparing heat out-doors by placing charcoal briquets in a can, in a garbage can lid, or in a wheelbarrow. Any of these home-fashioned barbecues serve the purpose as well as commercial barbecues. Their advantages over the commercial barbecues are that they are less expensive, and they provide a means of enjoyable creativity. The wheelbarrow makes a unique patio barbecue.

Principle

Use the outdoor can barbecue for stick, spit, aluminum foil, and grill cooking. The food is cooked by dry heat given off by coals or by charcoal briquets. The food will have a smoked flavor if the wood briquets are used.

Fire(s)

Charcoal briquets or coals are used for preparing food with this method. See the chapter on firebuilding for ways of preparing briquets for use. Crisscross or log-cabin fires will produce coals quickly.

Equipment Needs

Garbage-can lid and square can

Garbage-can lid or square can, pebbles, sand or dirt, and bricks. If a five-gallon can is to be used, tin snips and a hammer will be needed also.

Wheelbarrow

Wheelbarrow half filled with pebbles and sand or dirt.

One-gallon can

One-gallon can, aluminum foil, wire rack, and tin snips. Or: A number-ten can, a punch-type can opener, a can opener, a wire grill, a stick or a hanger.

Preparation

There are three major kinds of can barbecues: (1) the lid of a garbage can turned upside down, (2) a five-gallon can (such as a honey can) cut in half lengthwise and its sharp edges hammered down, and (3) a number-ten can.

To prepare either the garbage-can lid or the five-gallon can, follow these suggestions:

■ Place bricks under the lid or can if it is resting on a cement surface. If the garbage-can lid is used on dirt, dig an indentation in the dirt to fit the lid (fig. 82).

- Line the container with two inches of gravel, dirt, or sand so that the coals will not heat the metal.
- Pile the charcoal briquets on the gravel, dirt, or sand and light them, using a method suggested in the chapter on fire-building.
- Before you begin to cook, spread the briquets evenly over the prepared area. The briquets should not touch the galvanized part of the can because it may emit poisonous gases if burned.

One way to prepare a number-ten-can barbecue is to cut eight vertical lines one-third of the way down the sides of the can and bend back the metal strips to form a cup shape. Line the cup with aluminum foil, shiny side out, and add the charcoal briquets, covering them with a wire rack (figs. 83-85).

Another way to prepare a can barbecue is to cut both ends out of a can and place hot coals or briquets inside it. The food may be cooked on a rack on top of the can or with sticks or hangers.

Foods

Foods which can be cooked on a stick or spit or over coals can be cooked in a can barbecue. Foods which are oven-broiled can be barbecued, using the equipment described.

Steps

See the sections on stick, spit, and aluminum foil for both equipment and steps to follow. For grilling, a wire rack and rocks or bricks will be necessary to hold the grill above the coals. Refrigerator racks should not be used because they are covered with a toxic substance.

Fig. 82. Garbage can lid as a stove

Fig. 83. Number-ten-can barbecue

Fig. 84. Can barbecue lined with foil

Fig. 85. Place grill over foil

CAN OVENS

Can ovens are an enjoyable method of cooking. They are very good for the backpacker who wishes to "travel light," but they are usually small and should be used with groups of only two or three people.

Principle

Can ovens are used for baking foods. They are easily created by placing food inside one can or pan, then placing a larger can or other covering over the top to act as the oven. The trapped heat will circulate around the smaller can to bake the food.

Fire(s)

Coals are needed for can ovens. A log-cabin or crisscross fire will produce coals quickly, but charcoal briquets are also very effective.

Equipment and Preparation

The type of can oven you are making determines the equipment and preparation needed. Several types are suggested below.

Dutch oven can

A small can that fits inside another can or has a tight-fitting lid, like a dutch oven, can be used for baking. Special precautions should be taken not to place too many coals either below or on top of the can oven. Elevating the inside can on small rocks will regulate the temperature better.

Arch oven

A foil or can arch may be used to bake breads, pies, cakes, or any food to be baked in the oven of a range. The arch is dome-shaped to create a surface from which the heat will reflect. The arch may be made in several ways.

Foil arch. Place a wire rack over the hot coals and put the food on it. Make an arch dome from heavy-duty foil. Place it over the grill with the shiny side toward the food. Fasten the foil down with a green stick, or wire it to the grill before placing the grill on the heat.

Broiler-pan arch. Broiler pans wired or taped together in a teepee shape also work well as an arch (fig. 86).

Can arch. One half of a five-gallon can cut in half diagonally and laid down lengthwise may also serve as a good arch for an oven. Turn the sharp edges under with a hammer (fig. 87).

Fig. 86. Broiler-pan arch

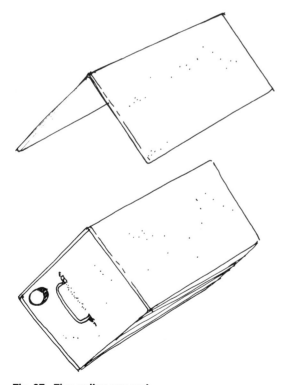

Fig. 87. Five-gallon can arch

79

Can over can

Set a can of cake batter or other food on three stones in the hot coals. Place a larger tin can over the small can. Place coals around the larger can and let the food cook as long as it usually takes to cook in an oven (fig. 88).

Meat can be baked using this same principle. Skewer or wire the meat to a heavy stick, then hammer it vertically into the ground until it stands up alone. Cut the top out of a five-gallon honey can, turn the can upside down over the meat on the stick, and push it into the ground to seal the oven. Place coals around the can and on top of it and cook the meat about 1½ to 2½ hours. Remove the can and check the meat to see if it is done.

Hang a can in a can

Use a one-gallon can, a small shortening can (or another can of that size) and a wire hanger. Cut both ends out of the gallon can. Punch three holes in the top of the small can with a punch-type opener. Push the sharp edges into the can, out of the way. Cut three wires four to six inches long. Make a hook on one end of each wire which will hook over the top edge of the one-gallon can and a hook on the other end that will hook the smaller can (fig. 89). Place the food in the small can and hook it into place inside the large can. Place the large can over the coals so that the small can rests about three inches above the coals. Cover the top of the large can with foil so that heat will circulate around the small can, creating an oven. Coals can be placed on the foil if more heat is needed.

With a slight variation, this type of hanging can may also be used for frying. Punch holes in the small suspended can, place briquets in it, and place a frying pan on top of the large can.

Round can oven

Place the food to be cooked inside a loaf pan. Suspend a larger round can over hot coals and cover its opening with aluminum foil to create the oven (fig. 90). Slide the loaf pan into the larger round can and let the food bake.

Five-gallon can or cardboard box oven

Cut the top and bottom from a five-gallon honey can or a cardboard box about twelve inches square and fourteen inches deep. Wrap the cardboard box with aluminum foil to protect it from burning and to create a greater amount of reflected heat.

coals or charcoal briquets

briquets

rocks

Fig. 88. Can over can oven

Fig. 89. Can in a can oven

flat rock

Fig. 90. Round can oven

Dig a small trench eight inches deep, eight inches wide, and about eighteen to twenty inches long. Place charcoal briquets in the can in one end of the trench and light them. (See chapter on fire-building on how to start charcoal briquets.)

Place one set of cross wires in the can or box. The set should be evenly placed six inches from the top of the box. The box is placed over the charcoal briquets (one briquet for every forty degrees of heat) in the open trench which extends from under the box and admits needed air to the coals. The edge of the box, even though it is reinforced with additional foil, should be kept away from direct heat as much as possible (fig. 91).

Place the item to be baked or roasted on the upper cross wires and cover the box with a roasting wrap (secured with either string or a rubber band) so that you can see the foods baking (fig. 92). Aluminum foil could be used, but it would not allow you to watch the food cooking. The oven can be lifted on and off the coals as needed. If desired, a portable oven thermometer can be hung on the upper inside of the box to determine the heat of the oven.

Dutch Oven

Dutch oven cooking is one of the oldest and is still one of the most popular types of cooking in the out-of-doors. A Dutch oven is probably the most versatile piece of cooking equipment available.

Principle

The Dutch oven is a piece of equipment that can be utilized in a variety of cooking methods. It is ideal for shallow frying, deep fat frying, roasting, baking, and stewing. Therefore, you may cook with either dry heat or moist heat.

Fire(s)

The Dutch oven is designed to be hung over open-flame fires, placed on the ground over coals, or buried underground in coals.

Open flame

A teepee fire or a lazy man's fire can be used when the Dutch oven is used as a kettle. The kettle is hooked to a tripod and hung over the open fire like a spit. It can also be hooked onto the end of a pole which is placed on a large rock, with another heavy rock anchoring it down at the other end (fig. 93).

Fig. 91. Cardboard box oven

Fig. 92. Bread baking in see-through oven

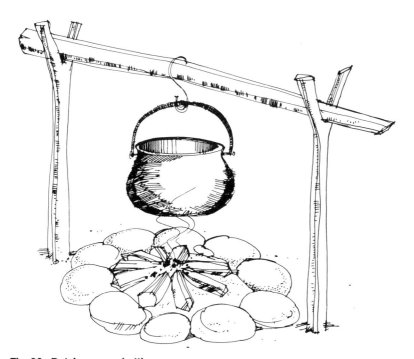
Fig. 93. Dutch oven as kettle

83

Fig. 94. Briquets for Dutch oven

Fig. 95. Briquets on lid of Dutch oven

Fig. 96. Stacked Dutch ovens

84

Coals

A keyhole fire is excellent because you can move the coals in and out of the cooking area as needed (see chapter on fires). A trench fire is very good, especially for the indoor Dutch oven, because the trench can be dug deep enough to keep coals from touching the bottom of the pan and narrow enough to rest the Dutch oven on the sides of the trench. This type of fire would be especially good for either shallow frying or deep frying because the kettle remains firm. A dug-out shallow pit, three to four inches deep, in which you make a bed of coals for the oven is safe and easy to make.

Charcoal briquets

If you are using charcoal briquets to make coals, place the correct number of briquets on both the top and the bottom of the Dutch oven, according to the following suggestions. A general rule is to leave about a two-inch square between briquets, forming a checkerboard pattern (figs. 94, 95).

Size of Oven	Top	Bottom
8″	6-8	4-6
10″	8-10	6-8
12″	10-12	8-10
14″	12-16	10-12
16″	16-18	12-16

Because charcoal briquets give off a great deal of heat, check the food periodically until you are sure how many briquets on both the top and the bottom will give you the right amount of heat for your Dutch oven. When you are using more than one Dutch oven, stack them in order to save briquets. Bake items in the lower ovens, and fry foods in the top one (fig. 96).

Underground

The Dutch oven works well in pit cooking for variety meals, one-pot meals, or stewing. See the section on pit cooking for further details.

Equipment Needs

The Dutch oven is a heavy, flat-bottomed cast-iron or aluminum kettle with a close-fitting lid and a sturdy handle. Varying in size from eight to sixteen inches in diameter and four to six inches in depth, it has heavy sides (about one-third inch thick) which hold heat evenly for a long period of time.

There are two types of ovens, the outdoor and the indoor. The outdoor oven has three legs, designed to hold the oven above hot coals and to allow air circulation below it. It has a relatively flat lid with a handle and with turned-up edges so that hot coals can be placed on it. The indoor oven is without legs so that it may rest on a flat stove. Its lid is round and without raised edges (figs. 97, 98). However, this oven can be converted for outdoor cooking by placing three similar-sized rocks or bricks under it or three to four ten- to twelve-inch spikes to support it above the coals (figs. 99, 100). To help the lid hold coals, make a foil ring just smaller in circumference than the lid (fig. 100). Set the foil on the lid and place hot coals inside the ring. The lid can also be turned upside down to hold hot coals.

If a Dutch oven is not available, a large kettle from a camp cooking set can also be used in many ways, similar to the Dutch oven; however, it will not hold heat as well and will burn more easily.

Care of Equipment

Although it is very heavy, the cast-iron Dutch oven can be broken if it is dropped or hit with something very heavy. Cold water on the hot oven might also break it or warp it. Thus, proper preparation and care of a Dutch oven is important.

Seasoning

Seasoning a cast-iron Dutch oven when it is new will help prevent rusting. Place the oven in the campfire or in your oven at home and warm it. Remove it from the heat and rub every area inside and outside with cooking oil or shortening. A cloth swab tied to a stick works well for this. Place the Dutch oven back in the fire or in your oven at 400 degrees for 20-30 minutes. Turn the oven off and do not open the door. Allow it to cool slowly. An old, rusty Dutch oven can be renovated by cleaning it well (see below) and seasoning it as just described.

Cleaning

Cast iron should never be scrubbed with soap and water or it will rust. Place a dirty Dutch oven on the fire, let the food burn off, and wipe it with an oiled paper towel. If your oven at home has a self-cleaning temperature, use that for cleaning a *cast-iron* Dutch oven.

Fig. 97. Dutch oven lids

Fig. 98. Dutch oven bottoms

Fig. 99. Spikes under oven

Fig. 100. Indoor-outdoor oven

Take care not to overheat an aluminum oven; it may melt. Aluminum Dutch ovens can be cleaned with soap and water so that seasoning is not necessary.

Preparation

A homemade Dutch oven, called a billy can, can be made easily from a number-ten can and a hanger or a heavy wire. Cut one end out of the can and punch two small holes on opposite sides of that end. Be sure to bend back the metal in the punched holes so that there will be no rough edges that might cut someone. Straighten out the coat hanger or wire and then curve it, securing the two ends to the holes punched through the can (fig. 101).

Foods

The Dutch oven can be used for cooking many different kinds of foods by several different methods. Frying and deep frying methods use heat only on the bottom. Baking, roasting, and stewing require an oven-type heat created by placing coals both on the lid and below the Dutch oven.

Steps
Deep-fat frying

- Place oil in the Dutch oven and set the oven over hot coals.
- If the oil heats up too much, remove it from the heat and cook in it until it cools.

Fish and chips, chicken, fritters, and corn dogs are a few foods that might be cooked in this way (fig. 102).

Frying

- The Dutch oven is excellent for frying food because it holds the heat well. Begin frying when the fat smokes in the oven or when water dropped on the iron sizzles.
- The lid to the outdoor Dutch oven can be converted to a shallow frying pan by hammering three or four spikes into the ground, placing coal under the lid, and putting the lid top side down on spikes (figs. 103, 104). Rocks or bricks may be used in place of spikes. The Dutch oven may also be placed upside down with coals or briquets placed on the bottom of the Dutch oven and the lid also turned upside down, resting on the legs of the Dutch oven (fig. 105).

Meat, eggs, and many vegetables may be cooked in this way.

Fig. 101. Billy can

Fig. 102. Deep-fat frying in Dutch oven

Fig. 103. Tall spikes

Fig. 104. Shallow frying pan

Fig. 105. Lid on Dutch oven legs

Boiling

Adjust the kettle above the coals. Move the coals around so that the water is at a slow boil rather than at a rollicking boil. The temperature of the water is the same at both stages of boiling, but when food is cooked at a vigorous boil, it will break up much more readily.

Stewing

- Brown the meat.
- Add the liquids and the vegetables.

With hot coals above and below the oven, this meal will cook without much more help from the camp cook.

Roasting

- Warm the oven first.
- Add suet or cooking fat and heat it until it begins to smoke.
- Sear the meat on all sides and slowly pour over it about ½ to 1 cup warm or hot water. Cold water will warp the oven. The water will allow the meat to be self-basting in the cooking process.
- Season the meat as desired.
- Cover with the lid.
- Surround the oven with coals.

This is a good method for cooking large pieces of meat. Vegetables may be added when the meat is partially done. It is best to cook at a moderate heat.

Baking

- Place a layer of foil, shiny side up, inside the Dutch oven.
- Place the food in the foil to bake it. This is a good way to bake cakes, upside-down cakes, biscuits, pies, and apples (fig. 106). Allow approximately the same amount of cooking time in the Dutch oven as you would in your oven at home.

For small cakes, shrink the large area in the bottom of the Dutch oven by placing rocks inside the kettle and forming heavy-duty foil over them, fashioning a smaller pan. Take special precautions not to puncture the foil, or the food will escape. If you have two foods in smaller amounts to prepare at the same time, place rocks in the center as dividers and make two foil pans inside the Dutch oven (figs. 107-9).

You may also use two pans in the Dutch oven. Cook together, for example, a meat loaf and scalloped potatoes or carrots (fig.

Fig. 106. Cake in foil-lined Dutch oven

Fig. 107. Shrinking Dutch oven area

Fig. 108. Dividing Dutch oven area

91

Fig.109. Area divided with rocks and foil   Fig. 110. Two pans in Dutch oven

110). Foods cooked in this manner should, of course, require about the same amount of cooking time; otherwise, they should be placed in the Dutch oven at different times.

Food can also be placed in a separate pan and set in the Dutch oven to cook. (Pies can be baked very successfully in this way.) Place four or five small flat rocks in the bottom of the Dutch oven to set the pan on. The rocks will elevate the pan so that heat may circulate around the food to cook it evenly and to keep it from burning (fig. 111).

Reflector Oven

Campers who roast or bake foods in a reflector oven will experience a real treat because it is one of the few methods of outdoor cooking where the cook can watch the cooking process.

Principle

A reflector oven operates with a concentration of dry heat. This outdoor method closely duplicates the process of the oven in your home: dry heat is created, then reflected from the walls of your oven around the food. Similarly, heat from the open fire is reflected off foil, metal, or rock into the oven and from the sides of the reflector oven (fig. 112).

Fig. 111. Pie baked in Dutch oven

Fig. 112. Reflector oven

Fire(s)

The best type of fire for the reflector oven is a teepee fire. If the wind is blowing, or if you do not have a fire with good flames, build a fire reflector on the side of the fire opposite the reflector oven. This will help reflect the heat from the fire back into the oven.

A fire or heat reflector can be built in any of the following ways:

- Build the fire close to a rock. The rock will reflect heat into the reflector oven.
- Stack up a wall of rocks to reflect the heat. The wall may need to be braced from behind by a heavy log.
- If two reflector ovens are available, place them across the fire from each other so that the ovens are facing. This will provide maximum reflection (fig. 113).
- Construct a heat reflector by placing two sticks securely in the ground side by side and stretching foil between them. If the shiny side of the foil is toward the reflector oven, there will be more reflected heat.

Equipment Needs

- Cardboard box: Aluminum foil, sticks or wires, large rocks or metal spikes, cardboard box.
- Foil reflector oven: Foil rack, sticks, rocks, or other brace.
- Cookie-sheet reflector oven: Five straight cookie sheets, metal rings, small bolts or wires.
- Sheet-metal reflector oven: Sheet metal, metal rings, aluminum foil, green sticks, heavy, stiff wire.

A reflector oven may be purchased or constructed at home or at the campsite itself. The purchased ovens usually fold up and transport easily, and some home-constructed reflector ovens can be made to collapse.

Preparation

The following are some different ways of constructing a reflector oven:

Cardboard box

A cardboard box lined with aluminum foil makes an adequate reflector oven. Use a square cardboard box cut in half diagonally and cover the inside of the box with foil — shiny side out to reflect the heat. Place green sticks or wires from side to side in the middle of the box to make a shelf, then cover the shelf with foil. Place a large rock at the back and a small one at the front to brace the oven in front of the fire, or use metal spikes (fig. 114).

Foil reflector oven

A reflector oven can be improvised from aluminum foil. Fold in half (with shiny sides together) a large piece of aluminum foil (about 24″ by 15″). Open out the folded foil until it forms a right angle.

Cut two pieces of foil to fit into each open end of the large piece of foil. Attach the end pieces by folding together the foil of the large piece and the end pieces.

Now find a rock or some other heavy base for the oven to rest on so that the open oven directly faces the fire. Set the item to be baked on a rack and place the rack horizontally into the oven, propping it at the front sides with cans or sticks or rocks. The heat will reflect obliquely from the foil oven downward and upward toward the rack (fig. 115).

If care is taken, the foil oven can be folded and stored in a pocket or pack to be used again.

Fig. 113. Two reflector ovens

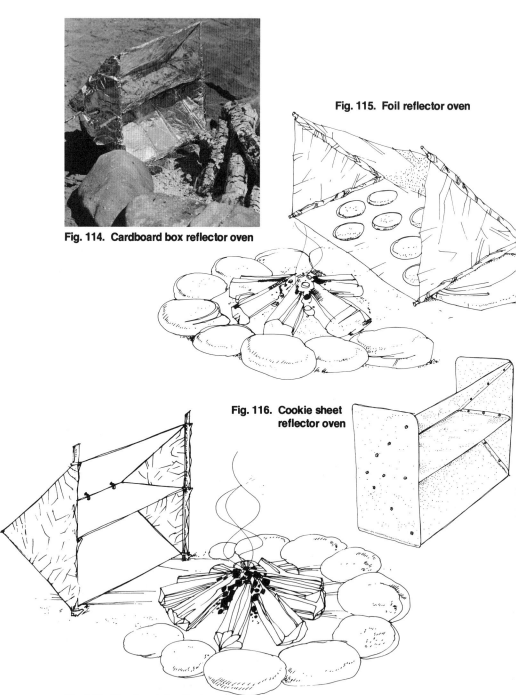

Fig. 114. Cardboard box reflector oven

Fig. 115. Foil reflector oven

Fig. 116. Cookie sheet reflector oven

Fig. 117. Sheet-metal reflector oven

Cookie sheet reflector oven

Five straight-edged cookie sheets can make a reflector oven. Three cookie sheets hinged together like a binder make the top and bottom of the oven and the center shelf. Bolt the sides of the top and bottom (which are at a right angle to each other and a 45-degree angle to the ground) to the sides of the oven, which are the fourth and fifth cookie sheets. Bolt the sides of the horizontal center shelf to the sides of the oven. The cookie sheet reflector oven is complete (fig. 116).

Sheet-metal reflector oven

Cut three rectangles of sheet metal of equal size and attach them together along one long side with metal rings, like a binder. Open out the three metal sheets so that the top and bottom sheets are at right angles to each other and the center sheet is horizontal. Holding each sheet in this position, lash each (with wire inserted through holes drilled in the corners of the sheets) to metal stakes or green sticks set in the ground on either side of the reflector oven. Cover the open sides of the oven with foil for additional reflected heat (fig. 117).

Care

Keep the reflector oven clean and shiny to create the most effective heat reflection. If the metal will not clean well, cover the oven with the shiny side of the aluminum foil outward so that it will reflect better.

Foods

Any foods that can be baked in an oven can be baked in the out-of-doors in a reflector oven. Cookies, brownies, biscuits, pizza, and cake are some of the favorites. Meats can be broiled quite easily also.

Steps

Place the food on a piece of foil or a pan which will fit on the shelf of the reflector oven, and place the oven near the fire. Knowing just where to place the reflector oven so that it will heat to the right temperature is the real key to cooking effectively. An oven thermometer inside the oven works well. Do not place it on top of the oven because it will catch the rising hot air and register a higher temperature than the shelf temperature itself. It is possible to learn to guess the temperature with reasonable accuracy by holding your hand just in front of the oven. If you can hold it there for only one or two seconds, the temperature is near 500 degrees. If you can hold it there for three to four seconds, 400 degrees; six seconds, 300 degrees; and seven to ten seconds, 200 degrees.

After the food has been cooking for five minutes, check it to make sure that it is cooking properly. Just lift the oven away from the fire area. Sometimes the food cooks faster at the front of the oven than it does at the back. If this happens, check to make sure that the oven is not too hot. Turn the food occasionally so that it will cook more evenly. If the top of the food is browning faster than the bottom, the fire is too large. Similarly, the fire is too small if foods are browner on the bottom than on the top.

Pit Cooking

Although it takes time and effort to dig the pit and prepare the coals and ingredients for pit cooking, after the food has been placed into the pit and has been buried, all of the hard work is done. Food wrapped in foil or leaves or placed in a Dutch oven cooks well in a pit. This is one of the few methods of cooking large items such as whole chickens, hams, turkeys, or roasts. By layering foods in the pit: meats, then potatoes, then vegetables, then even desserts, a whole meal can be cooked underground.

Principle

Heat is retained in the rocks and coals buried in the ground just as heat is retained in an oven at home. The main difference is the variation of heat. The pit starts very hot and gradually cools, while a commercial oven has a constant heat. Foods can be cooked to perfection in a pit even with this variance in heat.

Fire(s)

Build a crisscross fire which will produce many coals. Burn logs two to four inches in diameter. Unless you want an extremely hot pit to cook a turkey or a pig, logs larger than four inches in diameter will take too long to burn down. Add logs to the fire as it burns; many coals are necessary.

It takes about one hour to heat the rocks and to fill the pit with coals and ashes.

Equipment Needs

All that is needed to prepare a pit is a long-handled shovel and some flat rocks. Do not use rocks which retain moisture, such as rocks from stream beds or limestone or sandstone; they may explode.

Preparation
Underground Pit

- Dig a hole two to three times larger than the Dutch oven or the total size of the foil packages that will go into the pit. Remember that there should be room for rocks, and that the smaller packages of food should have two or three inches of coal between each of them.
- Line the pit with flat rocks.
- Build a fire in the pit and let it burn rapidly for at least an hour. The pit should be almost filled with coals and is now ready for the food to be placed in it (fig. 118).

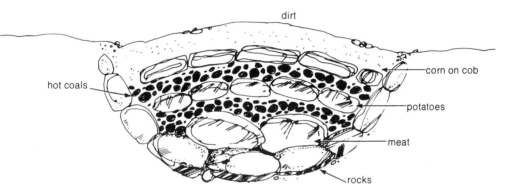

Fig. 118. Underground pit cooking

Above-ground Pit

If digging is not permitted or if the ground is too moist, prepare an above-ground pit by laying a base of flat rocks and surrounding that base with larger rocks. After building the fire and forming a large bed of hot coals, remove the coals, place the food on the rocks, and cover it with the coals. Cover the food and the coals with foil, and place about three inches of dirt over the entire pit (fig. 119).

Foods

This is excellent for complete meals including roast, ham, or poultry; potatoes, corn on the cob, and other vegetables; and desserts which can be cooked in a Dutch oven or wrapped in foil.

Chickens or turkeys can be stuffed if desired. So that flavors can cook through, the meats should be seasoned before wrapping in foil.

Many packages of chicken or other meats can be cooked in the same pit.

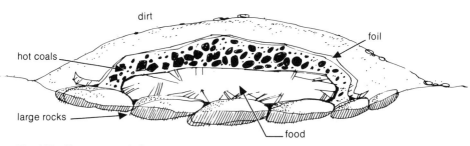

Fig. 119. Above-ground pit

Steps

- Prepare foods for the pit while the fire is burning down by wrapping them several times in aluminum foil. Food should always be placed on the shiny side of the foil, and the drugstore wrap should be used for sealing food. See "Aluminum Foil" section for directions.
- Remove the hot coals from the center of the pit and place them to the side of the pit. Do not spread the coals out any more than necessary because you will waste some of the heat.
- Place each wrapped item in the pit according to the length of time they require for cooking. Each item needs to be *completely* covered with coals. Two packages that touch each other will not cook well. Items requiring a longer time for cooking should be placed near the bottom of the pit, whereas those requiring a shorter cooking time will cook more slowly near the top surface of the pit. A thin layer of dirt may be shoveled over the coals between two items of food to cut down the heat. It will take practice to cook well this way because temperatures and times will vary depending upon the type of wood used and the number of coals you have.
- Cover coals in the pit with four to six inches of dirt. To make the coals emit hot steam, put wet burlap over the pit before covering the coals with dirt, or pour a can of water over the dirt. Also, a fire built over the pit would increase the temperature of the pit.
- Allow meat about the size of a chicken to cook from 3 to 3½ hours. Subtract or add time to this amount for smaller or larger items. Cut a large roast into smaller pieces to reduce cooking time.
- When the allotted time is up, carefully remove the food from the pit with a shovel. Be careful not to pierce or cut into the food packages. You will need gloves to help remove the packages because they will be hot. For easy removal of large foil packages, wrap them with wire long enough to protrude the top of the pit. This will assure location of the package when it is time to remove it and will prevent breaking the foil with the shovel.

Nonutensil Cookery

Nonutensil cookery consists of some of the most unique methods and demands great patience along with practice to master.

Cooking Food Inside of Food

A novel way to prepare some items of food is to cook them inside of other foods. Some foods will act as natural buffers against the heat while giving the foods inside additional flavor.

Egg or meat inside onion or orange

Cook an egg either inside an orange peel or an onion (fig. 120). Cut a lid off the orange or the onion and take out the center part, but do not remove the lid meat because it will add flavor. Break the egg into the peel. Set the lid on. If foil is available, wrap it in that. Or place it directly on the coals. Cook hamburger or other meats inside the onion by cutting the onion in half and removing about half of the inside (fig. 121).

Cake or muffin inside orange

Pour cake or muffin batter into a hollowed-out orange until it is about half full. Replace the lid of the orange, wrap it in foil if available, and bake it on the coals (fig. 122). The cake will have an orange flavor.

Fig. 120. Egg to be cooked inside onion

Fig. 121. Meat to be cooked inside onion

Marshmallows and chocolate inside banana (banana boat)

Cut a wedge-shaped section out of the length of a banana. Place marshmallows and chocolate chips or pieces of chocolate bars into the cavity of the banana. Wrap the banana boat in foil if it is available or place the banana directly on the coals. Other foods which can be placed in the banana boat are pineapple, maraschino cherries, and nuts (figs. 123, 124).

Heat Liquid in Paper

When liquid is heated in a paper cup or bag, the container will not burn. Because of this, water or milk can be heated in an un-waxed paper cup placed in the coals. Eggs can also be hard cooked in this manner (fig. 125). Milk can be heated in its carton if there is no wax on it. Small amounts of liquid may also be heated in a small paper bag. If the fire touches the top of the bag or cup where there is no liquid, the paper may become dry and will scorch or burn.

Breakfast in a Paper Bag

Use a small paper bag on the end of a pointed stick to cook your bacon and egg for breakfast. Cut the strip of bacon in half and cover the bottom of the paper bag with it. Break the egg into the

Fig. 122. Cake baked in hollowed-out orange

Fig. 123. Preparing banana boat

Fig. 124. Marshmallows and chocolate added

Fig. 125. Egg cooking in paper cup

104

Fig. 126. Eggs and bacon in bag

Fig. 127. Eggs and bacon cooking over coals in paper bag

sack over the bacon (fig. 126). Roll the top of the sack halfway down in one-inch folds and push a stick through the roll at the top of the bag. Hold the bag over the coals, and grease will coat the bottom of the bag as it cooks (fig. 127). The egg will cook in about 10 minutes. Be careful. If the sack gets too near the coals, it will burn. When the eggs and bacon are done, roll down the sides of the sack and eat your breakfast.

Novelty Cooking Methods

Outdoor cooking has its share of real novelty cooking methods, the possibilities of which are limited only by one's degree of creativity. One of the most exciting things that can happen in outdoor cooking is to create new, unique methods for cooking food.

105

After trying the following ideas, stretch your imagination and try to develop some of your own methods.

Cooking Directly on Coals

The direct heat of the coals will cook the food without any other equipment. It is best to use hardwood coals if there is to be direct contact with the food, because it creates a fire hot enough to burn the tars out of the wood. Softwood coals may leave a slight taste in the food, but use it if hardwood is not available.

Some foods are very tasty cooked directly on the hot coals. The following are only a few suggestions:

Toast

Place a slice of bread directly on white glowing coals (fig. 128). Turn over after about a minute. Before buttering the toast, blow and brush away the white ashes. Bread could be placed between folded foil and toasted in the same way.

Ash Cakes

From a stiff biscuit dough, make small flat cakes and place them on a bed of white ashes. Turn them when they are golden brown. A little brown sugar or jam in the center of two thin ash cakes makes a good pastry.

Fig. 128. Toasting bread on coals

Meats

If there is no other way to cook fish, steak, or hot dogs, place them over hot coals and cook. Fish should be cooked in the skin.

Rock Cooking
Method 1

Heat can be conducted through the rock from coal or fire below. Find a flat rock which is not over two inches thick. Rocks which have recently been in water or that retain moisture, such as shell and limestone, should be avoided because they may explode. Make a keyhole fire, brace the rock over the square part of the keyhole, and put hot coals under it. Heat the rock slowly. If one side heats too fast and expands more quickly than the other side, the rock may break. Turn the rock over and allow it to heat on the other side gradually and as evenly as possible.

When the rock is hot, it can be placed directly over the coals and used as a grill. When the upper surface cools, turn the rock over, brush it off, and cook on the hot side. If a rock is thin enough, the heat will be conducted through it and it will not need to be turned. The food may be cooked directly on the hot surface of the rock, or the rock may be covered with foil, as desired.

Method 2

Food may also be cooked on a round, hot rock with a smooth, flat side. It should be neither too large nor too thick and should be hard enough that it will not break, decompose, or explode when heated. Heat the rock in the fire, turning it occasionally to permit it to heat evenly, then remove it when it has become hot and brush the ashes away before cooking on it. Use it for cooking foods which can be fried quickly (fig. 129). When the rock cools, return it to the fire to reheat it.

Method 3

Small hot rocks stuffed inside meat will cook it. Using tongs and heavy gloves, first wrap the rocks in foil for cleanliness, then heat. Place one large hot rock in the breast of a chicken, for example, and a flat one under each wing (fig. 130). Baste the chicken with barbecue sauce and then wrap it in a foil drugstore wrap. Wrap the foil package in several newspapers for insulation, and finally, place the complete bundle in a plastic bag and tie it closed. Take the chicken on your morning hike. By noon it will be cooked. Hot rocks could also be placed in meat loaf or in other meats that could be wrapped around the rocks.

Fig. 129. Bacon cooking on heated rock

hot rocks

Fig. 130. Meat or chicken stuffed with hot rocks for cooking

108

Cooking in Sand

If you are cooking out on the beach or happen to build a fire on sand, the sand under the fire will grow hot enough to cook an egg. The sand acts almost like an oven. After a fire has been burning on sand long enough to heat it, move the coals off the sand and bury an egg for thirty minutes if you want to cook it until it is hard. After removing the egg, cool it in cold water if you are not going to eat it immediately. This will prevent a dark ring from forming around the yolk. Other easily cooked items, such as bacon, can be wrapped in foil and cooked, or the hot sand could be used as a warming oven.

Double Boiler

A double boiler cooks with the heat from boiling water rather than from direct heat. Foods easily scorched, such as milk, or foods which need to be cooked at a more controlled temperature are best cooked this way. If there is a need for a double boiler in camp, make one easily from two cans or pans, one fitting inside the other. Place rocks in the bottom of the larger pan and partially fill it with water. When the water is warm, place the smaller pan (or can) on the rocks inside the larger pan.

Dingle Fan Roaster

The dingle fan roaster is an old pioneer method of roasting meat. It operates on the principle that the fan will move away from the hot air and twist the string as it moves. As the string twists and unwinds, it turns the roast so that the meat is browned on all sides. It is also twisted by the action of the wind or a slight breeze.

Rest a long pole on a large rock with one end of the pole anchored to the ground by another heavy rock. The free end of the pole will rise into the air near the fire. To this end of the pole attach a length of chain about six inches long, then tie a heavy piece of string to the end of the chain. Tie a loop for a hook at the end of the string.

Using wire or a green switch, make a loop about nine inches in diameter and cover it with a bandana (by placing the bandana over the loop and tying the four ends of the bandana with string and drawing them together) to form the dingle fan. Tie the handle of the loop (two to three inches away from the fan) to the string just below the chain, and attach to the end of the handle (opposite the bandana-fan) a chunk of wood or stone to counterbalance the fan.

Tie the roast or chicken with wire or heavy string, placing one hook at the top and another at the bottom of the meat so it can be rotated. Place a foil pan under the meat to catch the drippings. Baste the meat occasionally until it is well done. Be sure to keep the fire burning; the hot air will keep the fan turning (fig. 131).

Toastite

The toastite, which may be purchased at many variety stores, is a novelty appliance consisting of two tongs attached to one handle that bring together two small, round metal discs. This method is similar to stick cooking over an open fire, except that a metal container encloses the food. Butter one side of two slices of bread and place the buttered side against each disc. Place a food such as pie filling, meat sandwich filling, or cheese on one slice of bread and close the tongs. Pinch off any bread around the outside of the metal discs and hold the container over the hot coals to toast (figs. 132, 133; colorplate 7).

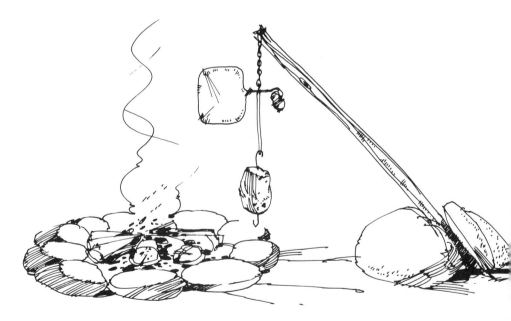

Fig. 131. Dingle fan roaster

Fig. 132. Filling bread

Fig. 133. Toasting filled bread in toastite

Oil Drum Stove

An oil drum will make a good stove. Cut a door from the side of the drum to place wood inside. Build a can or pipe chimney over the opening in the lid. The drum will probably need to be cut down somewhat. Build a fire inside the drum. The large metal surface will be as hot as an ordinary stove and can be used to cook on (fig. 134).

Manifold of a Car

While you travel, a novel way to cook food in foil is to use the manifold of your car. This is possible if you can find a flat area on the manifold on which to place the food so that it will not slip off. The food is cooked by heat from the pipe which carries hot air into the exhaust.

Place the food on the shiny side of a piece of foil and wrap it in the drugstore wrap. Wrap the foil package in a second piece of foil, also sealing it tightly to protect against juice leakage. Secure the foil package onto the manifold of the car and begin driving (fig. 135). The food will cook about as fast as it would at the medium temperature in a range oven, but you will have to watch it carefully the first time because the amount of heat will differ from car to car. When the food is about half cooked, stop and turn it over.

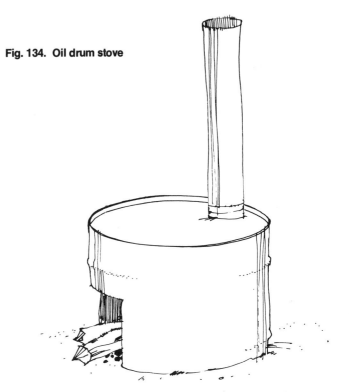

Fig. 134. Oil drum stove

Fig. 135. Cooking food on the manifold of a car

You may also heat soup or stew in this manner. This should be done only when the motor is not running, but immediately after traveling. Take precautions to puncture the can to prevent it from exploding.

Backpacker's Oven
Equipment
- Large size turkey roasting bag or square of some kind of roasting wrap eighteen inches square or larger.
- Heavy-duty aluminum foil at least three to four feet long and twelve to fourteen inches wide.
- Pliable, light wire (not galvanized) at least twelve feet long.

Procedure
Dig a small trench from six to eight inches deep, about eight inches wide, and fifteen to eighteen inches long. Place four twenty-inch, slender, green sticks securely in the ground in a ten-inch square at one end of the trench. These sticks should extend above the ground twelve to fourteen inches. String two sets of wires around the sticks and back and forth across the center of the square. The bottom set should be just above the ground level. Place on the wires inside the sticks a circular foil disk weighted down with small rocks. This disk will deflect the heat to the outside of the circle to make the oven temperature more even and to help prevent the food from burning. String the second set of cross wires five inches above the ground level. This upper set serves as a support for the item to be baked. Wrap the bottom of each stick with foil. Place the item to be baked on the upper wires (fig. 136). A baking pan can be made from foil. Stretch a turkey bag over the stick circle and over the outer wrapping of foil. You will be able to view the baking process and thereby judge the needed heat. Foil may be used instead of a turkey bag, but you will be unable to view the baking process. Heat is provided by hot coals from the nearby fire or from hot charcoal briquets placed under the oven through the open end of the trench. Heat can be increased or decreased by adding or removing hot coals or charcoal briquets.

A tin can stove may be used in place of the wires and the foil disk (fig. 137).

Fig. 136. Backpacker's oven

Fig. 137. Tin can stove in backpacker's oven

RECIPES

Planning

Meals at camp can be as interesting as they are at home if they are planned well. There are many factors to consider in planning for your group: tastes, amount of available money, methods of cooking. Other considerations are the duration of the camping trip, the mode of transportation, the number of people to cook for, and the sex and age of the campers. If marketing sources are unavailable for a week, fresh produce and meat are concerns; if the trip entails backpacking, heavy cans are impractical.

The key to planning good, practical meals for your camp is to choose your activities and plan your meals around those activities. For example, it is not good planning to have a breakfast which will take extra time to prepare if you want to start on an early hike.

Meals and Menus

The best and simplest guide available in planning daily menus is the Basic Four Food Groups defined by the Department of Agriculture. If this food guide is followed, it will form a basis for general good health at camp. Include the required servings of each group daily.

- Meat group: two or more servings for energy and growth. (Meats, poultry, fish, eggs, cheese, legumes.)
- Dairy foods: two for adults, three to four for children and teens for growth and body maintenance. (Milk, butter, cheese, other milk products.)
- Vegetables: one dark green or yellow vegetable.
  Fruits: one citrus fruit or tomato.
  Two other servings are recommended for good health.
- Breads and cereals: four or more servings for body regulation. (Breads, breakfast cereals, macaroni or noodles, and rice.)

Nutrition is always important. Involvement in outdoor activities consumes great amounts of energy and so requires careful planning for nutritious, well-balanced meals.

Breakfasts out-of-doors should be larger than other meals and full of energy foods. The lighter of the two remaining meals — lunch and dinner — could be a one-pot meal, a sack lunch, or hot dogs on a stick. Dinner is important because the bulk of the required foods will be planned into this meal.

Shopping
Use Charts
Very careful planning beforehand will save shopping time and will avoid wasted food. Purchase only those foods you have *planned* to use. The following three-step method should prove helpful to you.
- Chart 1: Plan carefully the menu for each meal.
- Chart 2: From the menu prepare a shopping guide of foods to be purchased.
- Chart 3: Write the amounts of each food you will need for each meal on this market order.

1. THREE-DAY MEAL PLANNER

	First Day Breakfast	Second Day Breakfast	Third Day Breakfast
Protein Food			
Cereal and/or bread			
Fruit or juice			
Beverage			
Utensils			

	Lunch	Lunch	Lunch
Main dish or salad			
Vegetable and/ or fruit			
Bread			
Dessert			
Beverage			
Utensils			

	Dinner	Dinner	Dinner
Main dish			
Vegetable			
Salad			
Bread			
Dessert			
Beverage			
Utensils			

2. SHOPPING GUIDE

Food	Weights/Approximate Measurement	Approximate Servings
Bread		
1 loaf	1 lb.	20 to 22 slices
Cereal		
Ready-to-eat:		
Flaked	18 oz./18 to 20 cups	18 to 20 1-cup servings
Puffed	18 oz./32 to 36 cups	26 1½-cup servings
Cooked:		
Oatmeal	18 oz./6 cups (1 cup uncooked = 1⅔ cups cooked)	12 to 14 ¾-cup servings
Rice		
Crackers		
Graham	1 lb./65 crackers	32 to 35 2-cracker servings
Saltine	1 lb./130 squares	32 4-cracker servings
Dairy Products		
Cheddar cheese	1 lb./12 to 16 slices 4 cups grated	6 to 8 sandwiches (2 slices each)
Cottage cheese	1 lb./2 cups	6 to 8 ¼-cup servings
Milk:		
Evaporated	14½ oz./1⅔ cups	Equivalent to 3⅓ cups milk. 1 can milk + 1 can water = whole milk
Whole	1 qt./4 cups	4 servings
Nonfat dry	1 lb./5 quarts	20 servings
Fats		
Butter or margarine	1 lb./2 cups	48 pats
Shortening	1 lb./2½ cups 3 lb./7½ cups	
Salad oil	1 pt./2 cups	
Flour		
All-purpose	1 lb./4 cups	
Whole wheat	1 lb./3½ cups	
Fruit Juices		
Frozen concentrated	6 oz./3 cups	6 ½-cup servings
Canned	46 oz./5¾ cup	11 to 12 ½-cup servings

2. SHOPPING GUIDE (Continued)

Food	Weights/Approximate Measurement	Approximate Servings
Fruits, Fresh		
Apples	1 lb./3 med.	3
Bananas	1 lb./3 med.	3
Grapefruit	1 lb./2 med.	2
Oranges	1 lb./2 med.	2
		1 orange = ⅓ cup juice
Pineapple	2 lb./1 med.	6 to 8
Meats		
Bacon	1 lb./20 to 24 slices	10 to 12 2-slice servings
Hamburger	1 lb./2 cups	4 to 5
General guide:		
Boneless meat	1 lb.	4
Small-boned meat	1 lb.	3
Large-boned meat	1 lb.	2
Chicken	2½ to 3½ lb.	4
Ham	1 lb.	4 to 6
Fish	1 lb.	2
Pasta		
Macaroni	1 lb./4 cups uncooked 8 cups cooked	14 to 16 ½-cup servings
Noodles	1 lb./6 cups uncooked 8 cups cooked	14-16 ½-cup servings
Spaghetti	1 lb./4 cups uncooked 8 cups cooked	14-16 ½-cup servings
Sugar		
Brown	1 lb./2¼ cups packed	
Granulated	1 lb./2¼ cups	
Confectioners'	1 lb./4 cups	
Syrup		
Corn syrup	1 pt./2 cups	
Honey	1 lb./1¼ cups	20 1-tablespoon servings
Molasses	1 pt./2 cups	16 2-tablespoon servings
Pancake	1 pt./2 cups	16 2-tablespoon servings

119

2. SHOPPING GUIDE (Continued)

Food	Weights/Approximate Measurement	Approximate Servings
Legumes, Dried		
All kinds	1 lb./2 cups uncooked 6 cups cooked	6 1-cup servings
Vegetables, Fresh		
Beans	1 lb./3 cups	5 to 6 ½-cup servings
Broccoli	1 lb.	3 to 4 ½-cup servings
Cabbage:		
Raw	2-lb. head/18 to 24 leaves	14 ½-cup servings
Cooked	2 lbs.	8 ½-cup servings
Carrots	3 mature/2½ cups	5 ½-cup servings
Cauliflower	1 lb./1½ cups	3 ½-cup servings
Lettuce	1 lb./1 large head	8 to 10
Onions	3 large; 4 to 5 med./ 2½ to 3 cups	
Potatoes	1 lb./3 med.	3
Tomatoes	1 lb./3 to 4	5 to 8
Miscellaneous		
Marshmallows	1 lb./64	
Peanut butter	18 oz./2 cups	8 to 10 2-tablespoon servings
Potato chips	1 lb.	16
Walnuts	1 lb./4 to 4½ cups	8 ½-cup servings

3. CHECKLIST FOR FOOD

Beverage
_____ dairy drink
_____ cocoa
_____ fruit juices
_____
_____
_____ tomato juice
_____
_____

Bread and Cereal
_____ bread
cold cereal
_____
_____
cooked cereal
_____
_____

Canned Foods
fruits
_____
_____
meats
_____
_____
soup
_____
_____
vegetables
_____
_____

Dehydrated & Dried Foods
_____ eggs
_____ fruit
_____ meat
_____ onions
_____ potatoes
_____ soup
_____ vegetables
_____
_____
_____

Cleaning Products
_____ soap for dishes
_____ soap for hands
_____ soap pads
_____ cleansers
_____

Condiments/Dressings
_____ catsup
_____ honey
_____ jam
_____ jelly
_____ mustard
_____ olives
_____ peanut butter
_____ pickles
_____ salad dressing
_____ vinegar
_____
_____

Dairy Products
_____ butter
_____ buttermilk
_____ cheese
_____ cottage cheese
_____ eggs
_____ margarine
_____ milk
_____ sour cream

Meat
_____ bacon
_____ beef
_____ chicken
_____ ground beef
_____ ham
_____ sausage
_____ steaks
_____ weiners
_____
_____
_____

Produce

_____ apples

_____ bananas

_____ celery

_____ carrots

_____ cucumbers

_____ grapefruit

_____ green peppers

_____ lemons

_____ lettuce

_____ melons

_____ onions

_____ oranges

_____ potatoes

_____ tomatoes

_____

_____

_____

_____

Paper Products

_____ aluminum foil

_____ bathroom tissue

_____ garbage bags

_____ kleenex

_____ paper cups

_____ paper plates

_____ paper sacks

_____ paper towels

_____ plastic bags

_____ plastic wrap

_____ wax paper

_____

_____

Miscellaneous

_____

_____

_____

_____

Cooking Time

Learning the cooking time for foods (when foods are done but not burned) is difficult at first but becomes easier with experience. In general, foods cooked out-of-doors should take about the same amount of time as foods cooked indoors. Foods cooked too fast run the risk of being either burned or cooked on only one side or of remaining raw in the middle. The chart on the following pages gives suggested cooking times and methods for recipes included in the book. The cooking time may vary according to amounts of food, altitude, and the degree of heat in coals.

Types of Wood

The length of time necessary to cook foods will vary with the type of wood; hardwood from broad-leafed trees makes longer lasting coals, providing a more extended cooking time than the softwoods from needlelike, evergreen trees.

Altitude

Water boils at 212°F at sea level. For every one thousand feet above sea level the boiling temperature drops two degrees. At 5,000 feet, then, water will boil at 202°F. Because of the lower boiling temperature at higher altitudes, foods take longer to cook.

Concentration of Coals

The amount and concentration or thickness of the bed of coals is also a determining factor for the length of the cooking time. The more concentrated the coals, the shorter the time for cooking.

Numbers in this chart (except those labeled *hr.* or *hrs.*) refer to cooking time in minutes.	Stick	Spit	Tin Can Stove	Aluminum Foil	Tall Can Stove	Can Oven	Dutch Oven	Reflector Oven	Pit	Nonutensil	Novelty
Breakfast											
Eggs and Egg Variations											
Soft and Hard-Cooked							10-20				10-20
Fried		5	5				5				
White Sauce							10				
Creamed							15-20				
Scrambled			3-5	3-5			3-5				
Eggs in a Basket			5	5			5				
Poached							10-15				
Bacon and Egg in a Sack											5
Bacon on a Stick	3-5										
Cereal							varies				
Overnight Breakfast							over-night				
Pancakes			3-5	3-5			3-5				
Cinnamon Toast	3-5			3-5				3-5			3-5
French Toast			3-5				3-5	3-5			
Lunch											
Special Stew							2 hrs.				
Sloppy Joes							20				
Campfire Sandwich				10							
Pizza							15-20	20			
Minute Pizza				10-15			10-15	10-15			
Pig in a Blanket	10						10	10			
No-fuss Lunch							15-20				
Bac-o-cheese Dogs	10-15							10-15			
Frank-a-bobs	5-10	5-10									
Dinner											
Meats											
Meat Loaf on a Stick	15-20	15-20									
Cannonballs				15-20			15-20				
Bunyon Burgers				25							
Meat Loaf				varies			60		3 hrs.		
Quick Meat Loaf								15-20			

Numbers in this chart (except those labeled hr. or hrs.) refer to cooking time in minutes.	Stick	Spit	Tin Can Stove	Aluminum Foil	Tall Can Stove	Can Oven	Dutch Oven	Reflector Oven	Pit	Nonutensil	Novelty
Meat Loaf in Cabbage				20-30		20-30	20-30				
Hamburgers			5	5	5		5				
Steak			varies	varies	varies		varies			varies	
Stuffed Zucchini				20-25			20-25				
Foil Dinner				25							
Hamburger Stew							60				
Tacos			15				15-20				
Beef Stroganoff							20-30				
Quick Macaroni Casserole							20-30				
Shish Kebab	10-20	10-20									
Camp Stew							45-60				
Stuffed Pork Chops							1 hr.		3 hrs.		
Barbecued Spareribs		1-2 hrs.					1 hr.				
Chicken Dinners											
Dutch Oven Chicken Dinner							45-60				
Chicken in Dutch Oven							45				
Chicken on a Spit		2 hrs.									
Chicken in a Pit									3-4 hrs.		
Fish											
Fried				varies	varies		varies				
Baked						30-40	30-40				
Steamed				20-30			20-30				
Vegetables											
Fresh				varies			varies				
Canned							varies				
In Foil				varies							
Potatoes											
Baked				1 hr.			1 hr.		1-3 hrs.		
Boiled							45-60				
Fried							20				
Scalloped						40-50	40-50				
Roesti							10-20				
Corn on the Cob	15			10-15			10-15				

Numbers in this chart (except those labeled *hr.* or *hrs.*) refer to cooking time in minutes.	Stick	Spit	Tin Can Stove	Aluminum Foil	Tall Can Stove	Can Oven	Dutch Oven	Reflector Oven	Pit	Nonutensil	Novelty
Hot Pot Green Beans							20				
Fried Tomatoes			5-10				5-10				
Camp Chili							20-30				
Baked Beans							1½ hrs.				
New England Baked Beans							5-6 hrs.		5-6 hrs.		
Quick Breads											
Biscuits Supreme						10-15	10-15	10-15		10-15	
Muffins			15-20					15-20			
Bread Twist	varies	varies									
Indian Fry Bread							5				
Twisted Donuts and Holes							5	5			
Crêpes							3-5				
Yeast Breads											
Hot Rolls							15-20	15-20			
Desserts											
Fruit Kebab	3-5	3-5									
Chocolate Pudding Cake							40-50	60			
Baked Apples				45-60		45-60	45-60	45-60			
Fruit Dumplings						20-30	20-30	30			
Pioneer Cobbler						25-30	25-30	30			
Pineapple-upside-down Cake		20					30-45	30-45			
Brown Bears in an Apple Orchard							25-45	25-45			
Cake in an Orange				10-15			15-20	15-20			
Cherry Delight		20				20	20-30	30			
Graham Cracker Cherry Pudding						20-30	20-30	30			
Easy Brownies						30-40	30-40	40			
Snacks											
S'mores	2-3								3-5		
Banana Boat				5							
Shaggy Dogs	2-3										

Substitutes

Sometimes, as careful as we are in shopping or packing, there are items missing. It is helpful to know how to expand meat with eggs, onions, and bread crumbs and how to expand eggs with bread crumbs. It is helpful to know what ingredients can be substituted for others. The suggestions in the following chart may prove useful.

- 1 teaspoon baking powder: ⅓ teaspoon baking soda plus 1 teaspoon cream of tartar.

- 1 cup butter: 1 cup margarine.
- 1 cup buttermilk or sour milk: 1 tablespoon vinegar or lemon juice in enough milk to make one cup; let stand for five minutes.

- 1 oz. (square) chocolate: 3 tablespoons cocoa plus 1 tablespoon fat.

- 1 tablespoon flour: ½ tablespoon cornstarch; 2 tablespoons quick tapioca.

- 1 cup honey: 1¼ cup sugar plus ¼ cup liquid.

- 1 cup milk: ½ cup evaporated milk plus ½ cup water.

- 1 cup evaporated milk: 1 cup double-strength powdered milk.

- 2 tablespoons onion: 1 tablespoon dried onion.
- 1 cup white sugar: 1 cup brown sugar.

Recipes

Because so many recipes are available to the public and adaptable to the outdoor setting, the purpose of this section is to acquaint you instead with some basic "tried-and-true" recipes and with ideas to help you adapt your own recipes to outdoor cooking. Each recipe is broken down into six or seven parts:

- *Its title.*
- *Cooking methods.* Many methods, including those you might create, may be used to cook the same item.
- *Cooking time.* The cooking time will vary greatly; so a rough estimate of the time is given, also a suggestion as to what constitutes "done" for each recipe. Check food often while you are learning.

- *Recipe yield.* The approximate number of servings is given.
- *Directions and ingredients.* Step-by-step directions are given at the left; ingredients for each step are shown at the right.
- *Variations.* Many items can be added to change the recipe, or the basic recipe may be prepared in several different ways. This list is by no means exhaustive. Your imagination can add many more variations to each recipe.
- *Hints.* Along with some of the recipes, helpful suggestions are given.

The recipes are categorized into the following areas:

Breakfast.

Lunch. The lighter meal of the day.

Dinner. Meats, vegetables, salads, breads, beverages, desserts. These can be used in lunch menus also.

Snacks.

Cooking without Recipes

To prepare foods without following specific recipes, it may be helpful to keep a few points in mind.

- In creating your own stew, always remember to brown the onions and meat first, then add water and each vegetable according to its cooking time — carrots and potatoes first, celery last.
- When you boil pastas (spaghetti, ravioli, or any fresh dough) or rice, remember to use about two times as much water as any pasta. Bring the salted water to a boil first and then add the pasta or rice. Add butter or oil to the boiling water so that the water will not boil over and so that the pasta will not stick together. Cover it and cook it at a low, bubbling temperature. For precooked rice, simply add rice to the boiling water, allow the water to return to a boil, then remove the pan from the heat and let it stand for about five minutes while the rice swells.
- Here are some general rules to follow:
Use one teaspoon of salt for each pound of meat; one tablespoon of baking powder for each two cups of flour; ½ teaspoon of salt for each cup of flour; two tablespoons of flour for each cup of liquid (for medium thickening); ⅓ cup of powdered milk (instant) for each cup of water.

Breakfast

Breakfast is essential; it supplies the body with the energy and nutrients it needs after it has been without food for ten to twelve hours.

Egg and Egg Variations

Soft and Hard Cooked

Method: pan, paper cup, or Dutch oven.

Time: Soft-cooked eggs — five to eight minutes; hard-cooked — twenty minutes.

Place eggs in water and bring to a boil. Remove from heat and cover. When eggs have cooked, remove and place in cold water.

Fried (colorplate 1)

Method: skillet, Dutch oven, and tin-can stove.

Time: five minutes.

■ Heat pan to medium heat.
■ Add   bacon grease or shortening.
■ Break in skillet   4 to 6 eggs.
■ Cook at medium temperature.

White Sauce (See following recipe.)

Method: skillet, pan, or Dutch oven.

Time: five to ten minutes.

■ Use following chart for
   desired consistency:

Thin	Medium	Thick	
1	1	1	cup milk
1	2	3 to 4	tablespoons flour
1	2	2½	tablespoons butter
¼	¼	¼	teaspoon salt
			pepper.

■ Melt   butter.
■ Add, stir together for few   flour
   minutes   salt.
■ Add and stir rapidly until   milk.
   smooth
■ Remove from heat.

Creamed

Method: skillet or Dutch oven.

- Prepare   2 cups medium white sauce.
- Dice and add to white sauce   4 hard cooked eggs.

Variations: Celery, ¾ cup diced; Cheese, ½ cup grated; Dried beef, ¼ lb. shredded; Sausage, 8 diced and browned links; Bacon, 8 strips, chopped and fried; Ham, ½ cup diced.

Scrambled

Method: skillet, Dutch oven, tin can, or aluminum foil pan.
Time: three to five minutes.

- Warm the pan.
- Add   bacon grease or shortening.
- Add   slightly beaten eggs and cook.

Variations: Add bacon (cut into pieces and fried). Sprinkle with grated cheese.

Eggs in a Basket (fig. 138; colorplate 2)

Method: skillet or tin-can stove.
Time: five minutes.

- Place in a "V" shape and fry   one slice of bacon.
- Place over bacon   bread which has a two-inch round hole taken from center.

- Gently press edges of bread down. Break into center of bread and cook on one side   one egg. Turn and cook other side.
- To give a french-toast appearance, lightly scramble egg in bread frame and draw it with a fork back over the bread.

Poached (fig. 139)

Method: Dutch oven.
Time: ten minutes.

- Place in Dutch oven and heat   2 inches of water.
- To keep eggs separated, place in water, bottom side up,   bottle cap rings.
- Pour inside rings   whites and yolks of eggs.
- Let cook until done.

Fig. 138. Eggs in a basket

Fig. 139. Eggs poached in jar rings

Fig. 140. Bacon on a stick

Bacon and Egg in a Sack

Method: paper sack.

Time: five to ten minutes.

- Cover bottom of lunch sack with 2 strips of bacon.
- Drop over bacon 1 egg.
- Roll sack down in one-inch folds and shove sharp-pointed stick through paper sack. Place over coals.

Bacon on a Stick (fig. 140)

- Punch hole in one end of 1 slice bacon.
- Slide upward onto stick, then wrap bacon around the stick and punch end of stick through other end of bacon.
- Toast over hot coals.

Cereal

Method: Dutch oven or pan.

Sprinkle cereal slowly into boiling salted water and stir constantly. Cook over medium heat until thickened. The following chart suggests cooking time for various cereals.

	Cereal	Water	Salt	Time
Cornmeal	1 cup	4 cups	1½ teaspoons	twenty minutes
Cream of wheat	1 cup	4 cups	1 teaspoon	ten to fifteen minutes
Rolled oats (quick)	2 cups	4 cups	½ teaspoon	twelve minutes
Wheat hearts	1 cup	4 cups	1 teaspoon	ten to fifteen minutes

Variations: Serve with butter and salt; honey; brown sugar; jam or jelly; sliced fresh fruit; raisins; dates; fresh berries; crisp bacon crumpled on top.

Overnight Breakfast

Method: Dutch oven in pit.
Time: overnight.

- Place in Dutch oven

2 cups oatmeal
1 cup dehydrated fruit
3 cups water.

- Bury Dutch oven in hot pit overnight.
- Dig up Dutch oven in morning. Breakfast is ready. May be served with

powdered milk or canned milk.

Pancakes (colorplate 2)

Method: grill.
Time: until golden brown on each side.
Yield: 12 to 14 pancakes.

- Sift together

1¼ cups sifted flour
1 tablespoon baking powder
1 tablespoon sugar
½ teaspoon salt.

- Combine

1 beaten egg
1 cup milk
2 tablespoons salad oil, melted shortening, or bacon fat.

- Add dry ingredients just until moistened (batter will be lumpy).
- Bake on hot griddle.

Variation: Use Bisquick mix and follow directions. Fruits or nuts may be added to the batter.

Cinnamon Toast

Method: reflector oven, over coals, aluminum foil in coals, on stick over coals.
Time: until bread is golden brown.

- Toast

slices of bread.

- While hot, spread with

butter or margarine.

- Sprinkle with

1 part cinnamon
4 parts sugar.

Hint: Keep cinnamon sugar mixture in a large shaker for easy use.

French Toast

Method: grill, reflector oven.
Time: until golden brown.
Yield: 10 slices

■ Combine in bowl
    3 eggs
    ½ cup milk or
        ⅔ cup canned milk
    ½ teaspoon salt.
■ Dip into egg mixture
    10 slices of bread.
■ Fry until golden brown in
    oil or margarine.

Variation: Roll bread (dipped in egg mixture) in cornflakes and place in Dutch oven. Cover with lid while cooking.

Lunch

Lunch needs to be simple, quick, and easily prepared, fitting in with scheduled activities. It is usually casual and informal.

Special Stew

Method: Dutch oven.
Time: 1½ to 2 hours.
Yield: 8 to 10 servings.

■ Combine
    ½ cup wheat
    ½ cup rice
    3 cups water.

■ Simmer until wheat and rice are soft. (Add more water if needed.)

■ Slice and add
    5 carrots
    4 potatoes
    1 teaspoon salt
    ¼ teaspoon pepper.

■ Dice and add
    1 onion.
■ Continue cooking until vegetables are tender.
■ Fifteen minutes before serving add
    4 beef bouillon cubes.

Hint: Soaking the wheat and rice together for two to five hours before cooking reduces cooking time.

Sloppy Joes
Method: skillet or Dutch oven.
Time: twenty minutes.
Yield: 7 or 8 servings.

- Brown

  1 lb. hamburger
  1 onion (diced).

- Add

  1 can chicken gumbo soup
  1 tablespoon catsup (or more)
  1 teaspoon mustard.

- Serve hot in

  hamburger buns.

Campfire Sandwich
Method: foil.
Time: five minutes per side.
Yield: 1 sandwich.

- Place on bun

  chipped beef
  slice of cheese.

- Place in

  foil.

- Warm in coals.

Variation: use other kinds of meat.

Pizza (colorplate 3)
Method: reflector oven, Dutch oven.
Time: twenty minutes or until brown.
Yield: 4 servings.

- Mix

  prepared pizza dough.

- Cut the size of reflector oven shelf and grease

  1 piece of foil.

- After dough rises, spread over foil

  1 tablespoon butter.

- Add

  tomato sauce, meat, cheese.

- Cook in reflector oven.

Minute Pizza (fig. 141; colorplate 2)
Method: reflector oven, Dutch oven, or foil pan on stick.
Time: ten to fifteen minutes.
Yield: 10 to 12 individual pizzas.

- Open

  1 can prepared pop-can
    biscuits or English muffins
  1 can pizza sauce.

- Slice

  1 pepperoni sausage
  cheese (10 to 12 slices).

Fig. 141. Minute pizza

■ Flatten and spread individual biscuits into round shapes on foil.
■ Put sauce, pepperoni, and 1 slice of cheese on each biscuit.
Variations:　Olives, green peppers and/or onions, other kinds of meat.

Pig in a Blanket
Method:　reflector oven, stick, or Dutch oven.
Time:　ten minutes or until golden brown.
Yield:　10 servings.

■ Prepare	Bisquick or canned biscuits.
■ Roll dough to ⅜" thickness.	
■ Cut dough into strips and wrap around	10 weiners.
■ Place over heat and cook.	

No-fuss Lunch
Method:　billycan or Dutch oven.
Time:　fifteen to twenty minutes.
Yield:　4 servings.

■ Boil	2 to 3 qts. water (will vary with amount of food to be cooked).
■ Place in boiling water (in order listed)	4 ears corn 4 wedges of cabbage 4 to 8 weiners.

Fig. 142. Bac-o-cheese dog

Variations: Other foods which have about the same length of cooking time can be combined in this way. If you don't want to mix flavors, purchase a special bag in which to boil vegetables.

Bac-o-cheese Dogs (fig. 142)
Method: stick or reflector oven.
Time: ten to fifteen minutes.
Yield: 6 servings.

- Cut lengthwise, but not completely through   6 weiners.
- Cut   6 small slices of cheese.
- Fill cut on weiner with small slices of cheese.
- Close weiner around cheese.
- Wrap bacon strip around weiner and cheese, and place toothpicks in each end.   6 strips of bacon
  12 toothpicks.

Frank-a-bobs (colorplate 4)

Method: stick.

Time: five to ten minutes.

Yield: varies.

- Cut in four or five pieces — 2 weiners per person.
- Open and drain — 1 can sliced or chunk pineapple.

- Thread frank onto stick, then add pineapple. Alternate this process until entire frank is on stick.
- Cook over hot coals.

Variations: Tomatoes, onions, green peppers, canned potatoes, cherry tomatoes.

Dinner
Meats

The main dish is the part of the meal that contains the protein and is usually in the form of meat. Basically, methods of cooking meat fit into two categories:

Dry heat includes roasting, broiling, and pan broiling and is used for cuts of meat without a lot of tough connective tissue. If dry heat is used for tough meat, the meat should be ground, pounded, or marinated in something such as French dressing before being used.

Moist heat methods include pot roasting, braising, and stewing. The meat is usually covered tightly and steamed to soften connective tissue. Tougher cuts of meat will tenderize if cooked with a small amount of acid such as tomato juice, sour milk, sour cream, or vinegar.

Fig. 143. Preparing meat loaf   Fig. 144. Cooking meat loaf on a stick

Basic Hamburger Mix

Methods and times are listed for each variation. Yields 4 or 5 servings.

- Combine in plastic bag

  1 lb. hamburger
  1 egg
  ½ teaspoon salt
  dash pepper
  ½ onion
  other spices as desired
  (bread or crackers may be
      added with some milk).

- Mix thoroughly.

Meat Loaf on a Stick (figs. 143, 144)

Method: stick or spit.

Time: fifteen to twenty-five minutes.

- Place on stick

  basic hamburger mix, one
      inch thick.

- Wrap tightly around the
  hamburger

  aluminum foil.

- Place over coals.

Variation: Strips of biscuit dough can be wrapped around meat.

Cannonballs

Method: foil, Dutch oven, or reflector oven.
Time: fifteen to twenty minutes.
Yield: 5 servings.

- Omit onions in basic hamburger mix.
- Cut horizontally in half   1 onion for each serving (5 per recipe).

- Scoop out the center half of the onion, both halves.
- Fill both halves with   basic hamburger mix.
- Place onions together and wrap, using the drugstore wrap.   aluminum foil
- Cook.

Variation: Could be cooked inside orange or tomato.

Bunyon Burger

Methods: in foil or skillet, Dutch oven, or reflector oven.
Time: twelve minutes per side.

- Shape into 10 to 12 thin round patties   basic hamburger mix.
- Place half the patties on   aluminum foil.
- Place on each patty   1 slice cheese
      1 slice pickle.

- Place another patty over the cheese and pickle; seal off edges of the two patties.
- Wrap in foil using drugstore wrap.
- Cook.

Variations: Other vegetables such as potatoes and carrots will cook very well in the center of the patties if they are finely sliced or grated. Onion slices can be placed outside the patties.

Meat Loaf (colorplate 4)

Method: pit or Dutch oven, or aluminum foil.
Time: pit, three hours; Dutch oven, one hour.

- Lay out   15″ × 18″ heavy-duty foil.
- Place on foil   2 cabbage leaves.
- Flatten to 4″ wide and 6″ long   ½ basic hamburger mix.

- Place on cabbage leaves.
- Place on mix   4 slices cheese.
- Top the cheese with the
  remaining meat.   ½ basic hamburger mix.
- Form into a loaf and cover
  with cabbage leaves.
- Wrap in drugstore wrap.
- Cook.

Quick Meat Loaf (fig. 145)

Method: reflector oven.

Time: fifteen to twenty minutes.

- Prepare in muffin tins or on
  baking sheet   paper cups.
- Place small amount in each
  cup   basic hamburger mix.
- Cook.

Fig. 145. Quick meat loaf

Miniature Meat Loaf in Cabbage Leaves

Methods: aluminum foil, can oven, or Dutch oven.

Time: fifteen to twenty minutes.

- Prepare in square pieces   aluminum foil.
- Divide into 8 to 10 portions   basic hamburger mix.
- Flatten each portion of mix and place half of them on   1 cabbage leaf each.
- Place in center of meat   1 slice cheese.
- Sprinkle with   1 tablespoon dried onion soup mix

  1 tablespoon water.
- Place another portion of meat over top.
- Close cabbage leaf and foil with drugstore wrap.
- Cook.

Stuffed Zucchini

Method: aluminum foil or Dutch oven.

Time: twenty to twenty-five minutes.

- Lay out, three to four inches longer than zucchini   aluminum foil.
- Prepare   basic hamburger mix.
- Clean and cut seed center out of   4 to 6 zucchini squashes.
- Stuff center of squash with basic hamburger mix and   grated cheese.
- Sprinkle grated cheese over top.
- Wrap aluminum foil in drugstore wrap.
- Place in coals or Dutch oven and cook.

142

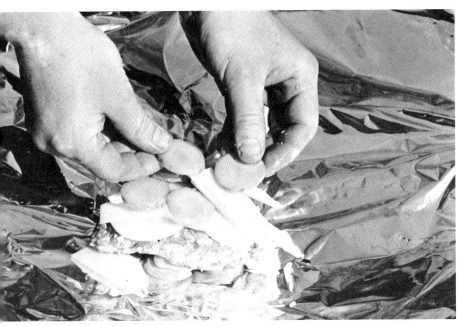

Fig. 146. Foil dinner

Foil Dinner (fig. 146)
Method: aluminum foil.
Time: twelve minutes per side.
Yield: 1 dinner per recipe.

- Place on table — 1½ ft. heavy-duty aluminum foil.

- Peel and slice — 1 carrot
  ¼ to ½ potato
  ¼ small onion.

- Form into patty — ¼ to ⅓ lb. hamburger.
- Arrange food in the following order: carrots, potatoes, onions, meat, potatoes, and carrots.
- Close foil with drugstore wrap.

Hints: If you do not use heavy-duty foil, wrap the dinner once, then cut three layers of newspaper to the size of the foil; roll them around the dinner, then place the dinner in a second wrap of foil.

Variations: Other foods can be added, such as tomatoes, green peppers, and pineapple.

143

Hamburger Stew

Method: Dutch oven or kettle.
Time: about one hour.
Yield: 10 to 12 servings.

- Brown

  2 tablespoons salad oil
  2 lbs. hamburger
  1 small onion, chopped.

- Add

  3 sliced carrots
  3 stalks celery
  2 cans stewed tomatoes or
  1 can tomatoes
  1 cup pitted whole olives
  ½ cup liquid from olives
  1 to 1½ cups pasta or rice.

- Cover tightly and cook.

Variations: Add, if desired, in order of cooking time: beans, hominy, corn, peas, cabbage, 1 to 1½ cups uncooked macaroni, noodles, rice, or soaked barley. For dumplings, mix Bisquick to muffin consistency and drop it on top of stew twenty minutes before serving. If desired add grated cheese just before serving.

Tacos

Method: Dutch oven, skillet, or tin can stove.
Time: twenty to thirty minutes.
Yield: 6 tacos.

- Chop and place in individual dishes

  2 stalks celery
  1 small onion
  1 head lettuce
  1 cucumber
  3 to 4 tomatoes
  ½ lb. grated cheese.

- Fry in hot

  fat
  1 lb. hamburger (or ½ lb. pork and ½ lb. hamburger).

- Place skillet over heat and leave until hot, then add

  ¼ lb. oil or fat.

- Dip and cook in hot fat until soft

  12 tortillas.

- Place on plates: tortillas, meat, vegetables, cheese.

- Sauces may be desired: taco sauce, catsup, salad dressing, etc.
- Close tortillas and serve while hot.

Variation: Make Indian fry bread and place beans and meat on bread, also other foods as desired (fig. 147).

Beef Stroganoff

Methods: Dutch oven or kettle.

Time: simmer ten to fifteen minutes; noodles twenty to thirty minutes.

Yield: 6 servings.

- Boil and cook until done
  2 cups uncooked egg noodles
  1 teaspoon salt
  few drops oil.

- Brown
  1 lb. hamburger
  1 onion.

- Add
  1 can cream of mushroom soup
  ½ can milk
  pepper to taste.

- Simmer.
- Serve over cooked noodles.

Variations: sour cream, parsley, Worcestershire sauce, mushrooms.

Fig. 147. Taco

Quick Macaroni Casserole

Method: skillet or Dutch oven.
Time: twenty to thirty minutes.
Yield: 5 or 6 servings.

- Melt
- 2 tablespoons margarine or butter.

- Sauté
- ¼ cup chopped onion
- ¼ cup chopped green pepper.

- Add and cook until brown
- ½ lb. ground beef.
- Add
- 1 can chicken gumbo soup
- 1 can cream of chicken soup
- ¾ to 1¼ cup water
- 1 teaspoon water
- 1 teaspoon salt
- ⅛ teaspoon pepper.

- Gradually stir in
- 2 cups uncooked macaroni.
- Cover and cook until macaroni is tender.

Hint: If liquid thickens too much, add water to right consistency.

Shish Kebab (colorplate 4)

Method: stick or spit.
Time: ten to twenty minutes.
Yield: 5 or 6 servings.

- Marinate or precook to speed up cooking time
- 1 lb. small chunks of meat.

- With the meat, alternate on skewer

chunks of pineapple
canned potatoes
onions
cherry tomatoes
slices of green pepper.

- It may be necessary to thread meat through twice so it turns with the stick.
- Cook over the hot coals until done.

Variation: Brush with barbecue sauce if desired.

Hint: To marinate meat, cut into chunks and place in mixture of two parts oil and one part vinegar. Herbs and seasoning may be added for flavor. (Purchase a packaged seasoning for salad dressing and add.) Let stand twenty-four hours in a cool place.

146

Camp Stew

Method: Dutch oven, kettle, or skillet.

Time: forty-five minutes to one hour.

Yield: 5 or 6 servings.

- Brown in pan   1 lb. meat, cubed.
- Stir in and simmer until done   1 can stewed tomatoes
                                                        1 can corn or hominy.

- If desired, add just before
  serving   ¼ lb. sliced cheese.

Variations: Other raw or canned vegetables may be added as desired. If a thickened gravy is desired, add flour mixed with cold water.

Stuffed Pork Chops

Method: pit, skillet, or Dutch oven.

Time: about one hour (two to three hours in pit).

Yield: 6 servings.

- Prepare stuffing   ½ loaf bread
                                                        2 or 3 eggs
                                                        2 stalks celery
                                                        sage, thyme to flavor
                                                        1 teaspoon salt
                                                        (milk as needed for desired
                                                            moistness).

- Stuff center of   6 pork chops (thick, filleted).
      or
  place stuffing in bottom
  of pan and place pork chops
  on top.
- Cook.

Variation: Lamb chops can be used.

Barbecued Spareribs

Method: Dutch oven or kettle and barbecue.

Time: Boil one hour; barbecue until warm and brown.

Yield: any number desired.

- Boil   desired number of spareribs
                                                        (country style are best)
                                                        water to cover
                                                        1 small clove garlic
                                                        salt to taste.

- Drain and set aside until about time to eat.
- Place meat in bowl and cover with
- Place on barbecue rack.
- Cook until done, turning so they will not burn.

commercial barbecue sauce.

Chicken Dinners
Dutch Oven Chicken Dinner
Method: Dutch oven.
Time: forty-five minutes.
Yield: 4 or 5 servings.
- Cut into pieces
- Shake in sack of

1 chicken.
flour
spices as desired.
hot butter.

- Place in Dutch oven in
- Brown chicken.
- Place around pieces
- Add over top

2 sliced onions.
4 sliced potatoes
4 sliced carrots
½ cup water.

- Cover and let steam until tender.

Chicken in Dutch Oven
Method: Dutch oven.
Time: forty-five to sixty minutes.
Yield: 5 or 6 servings.
- Mix and place in bottom of Dutch oven (soup undiluted)

1 can cream of mushroom
   soup
1 can cream of celery soup
1 can cream of chicken soup
2 cups white rice.

- Place on top
- Sprinkle
- Place Dutch oven in coals and cook.

1 cut-up chicken.
½ pkg. dried onion soup.

Bacon and eggs

Minute pizza

Eggs in a basket

Sourdough pancakes

Colorplate 2

Pizza

Kebabs

Meat loaf   **Colorplate 4**

Chicken on a spit   Corn on the cob   Bread twist

Watermelon salad

Pineapple upside-down cake

Cake in an orange

Cherry delight

Cherry pie in toastite

Colorplate 7

155

Sourdough biscuits

Sourdough bread   Colorplate 8

156

Chicken on a Spit (colorplate 5)

Method: spit.
Time: 1½ to 2 hours.

- Place on spit and wire tightly   1 chicken.
- Brush with   barbecue sauce.
- Place 1½ feet above coals
  and cook until done, turning
  about every five minutes.

Chicken in Pit

Method: pit.
Time: three to 3½ hours
Yield: 4 or 5 servings.

- Mix together   ½ loaf bread
  1 stalk celery, cut up
  1½ teaspoons sage
  1 teaspoon salt
  1 egg
  1 grated carrot
  ½ cup milk
  ½ teaspoon pepper.
- Stuff   1 chicken.
- Spread well on outside of
  chicken   butter.
- Add   salt and pepper.
- Wrap chicken tightly in three
  or four layers of 24″ × 24″
  heavy-duty foil, using
  drugstore wrap. Newspapers
  may be used instead of extra
  layer of foil.
- Bury in pit.

Fish

Fish can be baked in foil, fried in skillet, fried or baked in Dutch oven.

Fried

Method: Dutch oven or skillet.
Time: varies (cook over medium-low heat until tender).

- Flour fish and place in buttered skillet.
- Cook until tender.

Baked

Method: Dutch oven or can oven.
Time: thirty to forty-five minutes.
- Follow step #1 for fried fish.
- Add small amount of water, tomato juice, or milk.
- Cover with lid and place in hot coals.

Steamed

Method: foil.
Time: ten minutes per side for medium fish.
- Place fish on piece of foil large enough to seal in drugstore wrap.
- Place in coals.
- Cook.

Vegetables

The main concern in preparing and cooking vegetables is to retain food value. For example, most vegetables are rich in minerals just under the skin; therefore, whenever possible, peelings should remain on the vegetables. Do not soak vegetables in cold water before cooking since soaking sometimes increases loss of vitamins.

Other points to remember in boiling vegetables: (1) boil steadily, but not rapidly, as rapid boiling dissolves food nutrients; (2) always cover the pan in cooking; (3) cook until just underdone; (4) use a small amount of water and then use the water from vegetables for gravies or soups whenever possible.

Fresh

Method: foil, Dutch oven, or kettle.
Time: cook until tender.
- Place in pan   ¼ to 1 cup water.
- Add   fresh vegetables.

Variations: Any vegetable can be used.

Canned

Method: can, Dutch oven, or kettle.
Time: twenty minutes, or until well heated. Varies with amount of food.
- Puncture or open   1 can vegetables.
- Place over coals to heat.

Variation: When using Dutch oven or pan, use lid and place in coals.

In Foil

Method: foil.

Time: about the same amount of time as at home (this will vary with kind and amount of food).

- Place on squares of foil   vegetables.
- Roll in drugstore wrap.
- Add   2 to 4 tablespoons water, oil,
- Cook.   or butter.

Potatoes
Baked

Method: foil, Dutch oven, or pit.

Time: in hot coals, one hour; in pit, for the length of time food is to be buried.

- Clean potatoes (butter them if desired) and wrap in piece of foil, using drugstore wrap.
- Place in coals to cook.

Boiled

Method: Dutch oven or pan.

Time: forty-five minutes to one hour, until tender.

- Place water in pan and bring to boil.
- Clean potatoes; peel if desired.
- Place potatoes in boiling water in one of the following forms: whole, quartered, sliced.
- Cook until tender.

Variations: Boiled potatoes can be used for mashing, for creaming with peas (make cream sauce or warm potatoes with cream of mushroom soup), for making potato salad, or for chopping and frying.

Fried

Method: Dutch oven or skillet.

Time: ten to twenty minutes.

Method 1.   Peel and grate (or finely chop or slice) raw potatoes. Place in pan with 2 tablespoons butter. Fry until golden brown and crisp.

Method 2.   Peel and dice precooked potatoes. Place in skillet with about 2 tablespoons butter, and fry them.

Scalloped

Method: Dutch oven or can oven.

Time: one hour.

Yield: 6 to 8 servings.

- Peel and thinly slice   4 or 5 raw potatoes.
- Finely chop   1 onion.
- Mix together well   1 can mushroom soup

                                               1 can milk.

- Layer the ingredients: a few potatoes, a few onions, and some soup mixture.
- Dot with   butter.
- Layer again.
- Top may be sprinkled with   bread crumbs.

Roesti (Swiss Potato)

Method: Dutch oven or skillet.
Time: ten to twenty minutes or until brown.
Yield: 5 to 6 servings.

- Cut and cook   6 strips of bacon.
- Dice and add   1 onion.
- Cook until tender.
- Grate and add   2 precooked potatoes.
- Place in pan and fry.

Corn on the Cob (colorplate 5)

Method: foil or stick.
Time: five minutes per side.

- Pull down husk and remove cornsilk from   ear of corn.
- Dot with   1 teaspoon butter.
- Add   dash of salt.
- Sprinkle with   water.
- Replace husk.
- Wrap with   foil.
- Place in coals.

Variations: Barbecue sauce or chili powder can be added. Corn may be placed on a stick and cooked over coals.

Hot Pot Green Beans

Method: Dutch oven or pan.
Time: twenty minutes.
Yield: 8 servings.

- Place in pot   2 cans French-cut green beans (drained).

- Add   1 can cream of mushroom soup
  ½ can milk or water
  2 tablespoons dry onion flakes.

- Place in coals and bake until hot.

Variations: Add slivered almonds or ½ cup cashew nuts.

Fried Tomatoes
Method: skillet or grill, tin can stove, Dutch oven.
Time: five to ten minutes, until warmed through.

- Slice thinly   green or not-too-ripe tomatoes.
- Place slices in   flour.
- Place in   hot grease.
- Cook; turn and season with   salt and pepper.
- Serve hot.

Camp Chili
Method: Dutch oven or pan.
Time: twenty to thirty minutes.
Yield: 6 to 8 servings.

- Brown in skillet   1 lb. hamburger
  1 diced onion.

- Drain off excess fat.
- Add   1 large can kidney beans or red beans
  1 can cream of tomato soup
  2 teaspoons chili powder
  salt and pepper to taste.

- Simmer together.

Variation: can be served over hamburger or hot dog buns.

Baked Beans
Method: Dutch oven.
Time: 1½ hours.
Yield: 10 servings.

- Cut and brown in skillet   ½ lb. bacon
  ½ large onion.

- Combine in skillet   1 large can pork and beans
  ½ large green pepper, chopped

4 oz. catsup
½ cup brown sugar
1 tablespoon Worcestershire
sauce
1½ teaspoons vinegar.

- Place in coals and cook.

Variations: Use weiners. For sweet and sour add 1 can pineapple chunks and juice and 2 tablespoons molasses.

New England Baked Beans

Method: Dutch oven or pan in a pit.
Time: 5 to 6 hours.
Yield: 8 servings.

- Soak overnight, then simmer until the skins begin to break   1½ lbs. dried beans (3 cups)
5 cups water.
- Add
1 medium onion, chopped
1 tablespoon salt
1 cup brown sugar
2 tablespoons molasses
2 teaspoons dry mustard
1½ cups ketchup
½ lb. bacon cut in cubes.
- Cover ingredients with   water.
- Cover pan and bake in pit.

Salads

Salads are an important part of the outdoor menu and should not be overlooked. They add color, variety, and nutrition to the meal.

Tossed Green Salad

- Break into bite-sized pieces   1 head lettuce.
- Dice or slice   2 or 3 tomatoes.
- Combine.
- Serve with   favorite dressing.

Variations: cucumbers, carrots, celery, green peppers, cherry tomatoes, avocados, sliced eggs, tuna, cheese, shrimp, or a variety such as in a chef's salad.

Macaroni Salad

Method: Dutch oven or kettle.
Time: twenty minutes cooking; ten minutes mixing.

Yield:　6 to 8 servings.

■ Cook, drain, and cool

1 cup uncooked macaroni
(about 2 cups cooked).

■ Dice

½ cup celery
2 sweet pickles
3 hard-cooked eggs.

■ Add

1 can tuna
½ to ¾ cup salad dressing
thinned with milk
½ teaspoon mustard
½ teaspoon sugar
salt to taste.

■ Combine and serve.

Variations:　shrimp, crab, cooked peas, green pepper, cucumbers.

Potato Salad

Method:　Dutch oven or kettle.
Time:　forty-five minutes cooking; ten minutes mixing.
Yield:　8 to 10 servings.

■ Boil and dice

6 to 8 medium-sized potatoes
4 to 6 eggs.

■ Chop

1 cup celery
2 to 3 medium green onions.

■ Mix

¾ to 1 cup salad dressing
thinned with canned milk.

■ Combine all ingredients.　salt and pepper to taste.

Variations: pickles, other vegetables, mustard or catsup in dressing.

German Potato Salad (Hot Potato Salad)

Method:　skillet.
Time:　forty-five minutes cooking; fifteen minutes preparing.
Yield:　6 to 8 servings.

■ Cook until crisp, drain, and
crumble

½ lb. bacon.

■ Cook in bacon fat until tender　½ cup chopped onion.

■ Blend in

2 tablespoons flour
2 tablespoons sugar
1½ teaspoons salt
1 teaspoon celery seed
½ cup vinegar.

■ Stir until thickened and bubbly.

- Add

6 cups diced cooked potatoes
2 hard-cooked eggs, diced
bacon.

- Heat thoroughly, tossing
  lightly.
- Garnish with

parsley
pimento
bacon curls.

Cole Slaw
Time: ten minutes.
Yield: 6 to 8 servings.

- Finely chop

½ head cabbage.

- Mix together

½ cup mayonnaise
1 to 2 tablespoons canned milk
1 teaspoon sugar (optional).

- Mix and pour over cabbage.

Variations: ½ cup salted peanuts, 1 small can crushed pine-apple, ½ cup raisins, diced green peppers and tomatoes; or add sour cream to the dressing mixture.

Jello Salad
Time: overnight; ten minutes preparing.
Yield: 6 servings.

- Prepare

1 pkg. Jello, any flavor.

- Add

fruit or other filler as desired.

- Place in container which
  can be tightly covered.
- Place in creek overnight.
  Salad will be set.

Waldorf Salad
Time: twenty minutes preparing.
Yield: 6 to 8 servings.

- Dice or chop

4 apples
3 stalks celery
½ cup nuts.

- Combine for dressing

½ cup mayonnaise
1 to 2 tablespoons sugar
milk to thin or
1 pkg. whip-cream substitute,
  mixed.

164

- Add dressing to chopped ingredients.
- Mix well.

Watermelon Salad (colorplate 5)

Time: thirty minutes preparing.

Yield: 10 to 12 servings.

- Slice in half lengthwise
- Ball
- Add and mix well

1 watermelon.
watermelon and cantaloupe.
1 large can fruit cocktail
3 or 4 bananas, sliced.

- Place mixture into watermelon shells to serve.

Hints: For fancy watermelon serving dish, cut melon halves in scallops or zigzag. Fruit can be arranged in many decorative ways.

Variations: other fruits, nuts, maraschino cherries.

Breads

Breads are a very popular item at camp. The two different types of breads are quick breads and yeast breads. Quick breads are made with baking powder and can be prepared in a short period of time. On the other hand, breads leavened by yeast require warm weather and an entire morning or afternoon to prepare.

Quick Breads

Biscuits Supreme

Method: reflector oven, Dutch oven, can oven, or on coals as ash cakes.

Time: ten to fifteen minutes or until just turning brown.

Yield: 12 biscuits.

- Sift into bowl

2 cups flour
½ teaspoon salt
3 teaspoons baking powder
½ teaspoon cream of tartar
2 teaspoons sugar.

- Cut in until mixture resembles crumbs
- Add and stir with fork
- Knead lightly.
- Roll ½ inch thick and cut with biscuit cutter or open-end can.
- Bake.

½ cup shortening.
⅔ cup milk.

Muffins

Method: reflector oven, tin can stove.
Time: fifteen to twenty-five minutes, until golden brown.
Yield: 12 muffins.

- Sift into bowl

2 cups white or whole wheat
  flour
3 teaspoons baking powder
½ teaspoon salt
¼ cup sugar.

- Make a well in dry ingredients.
- Combine and pour into well

1 egg
1 cup milk or ⅓ cup powdered
  milk combined with
  1 cup water
¼ cup melted fat or oil.

- Stir twenty strokes with fork
  (only until dry ingredients are
  dampened). Batter will not be
  smooth.
- Fill

muffin pans or individual cups
  made from foil.

- Bake.
- Serve hot.

Variations:

- Bacon: Substitute 4 tablespoons bacon drippings for butter or margarine. Add bacon drippings and 3 tablespoons chopped crisp bacon to egg-milk mixture.
- Blueberry: Add 1 cup blueberries after liquid and dry ingredients have been mixed. Add 4 additional tablespoons of sugar, if desired.
- Cornmeal: Substitute 1 cup cornmeal for 1 cup flour. Substitute ½ teaspoon baking soda for 1 teaspoon baking powder and 1 cup sour milk for 1 cup sweet milk.
- Date: Add ½ cup chopped pitted dates to sifted flour mixture.
- Orange: Substitute ½ cup orange juice for ½ cup milk. Add orange juice and 1 teaspoon grated orange rind to egg mixture.

Bread Twist (colorplate 5)
Method: stick or spit.
Time: until brown.

Method 1: Stick Biscuits

■ Shape into thin strips and wrap around stick refrigerator biscuits.

■ Cook over hot coals.

Method 2: Thumbprint Bread (figs. 148, 149)

■ Cut a "V" on side of   1 Bisquick box.

■ Peel triangular section back.

■ Make a well in Bisquick.

■ Pour into well   1 tablespoon water.

■ With end of stick, stir until soft dough forms around stick.

■ Bisquick dough can then be molded around the stick.

■ Cook over hot coals.

Recipe by Norman C. Roan.

Fig. 149. Prepared thumbprint bread

Fig. 148. Preparing thumbprint bread

167

Fig. 150. Oiling end of stick

Fig. 151. Molding bread dough over stick

Fig. 152. Baking bread cup over coals

168

Bread Cup on a Stick (figs. 150-52)
Method: stick about two inches in diameter.
Time: ten to twenty minutes.
- Grease end of stick with   shortening or oil.
- Make a dough, mold over end
  of stick   dough.
- Brown over coals until done.
- Pull off stick and spoon stew
  inside.

Method 4:   Dough Boy
- Mix a stiff dough   Bisquick
  water.

- Form dough into snakelike
  coil.
- Wrap coil around stick.
- Cook slowly over coals.
  Serve any of the above with honey, jam, or butter in the cavity
left when the stick is removed.

Indian Fry Bread
Method: Dutch oven.
Time: five minutes cooking.
Yield: 20 to 24.
- Mix well   4 cups flour
  1 tablespoon salt
  1 tablespoon baking powder.
- Add until mixture forms stiff   water.
  dough
- Knead until dough is thick and
  elastic.
- Form into very thin round
  patties.
- Fry in ½ inch grease or oil
  until brown on each side.

Twisted Donuts and Holes

Method: reflector oven, can oven.
Time: ten to fifteen minutes, until just browning.

- Mix thoroughly, then beat vigorously twenty strokes

    2 cups Bisquick
    2 tablespoons sugar
    1 teaspoon nutmeg
    ⅛ teaspoon cinnamon
    ⅓ cup milk
    1 egg.

- Place on   board.
- Knead five times.
- Roll ½-inch thick.
- Cut with   floured doughnut cutter.
- Twist donut by holding opposite sides and turn to make figure eight.
- Place figure eights and dough from holes on ungreased baking sheet.
- Bake.
- Immediately after baking, dip each into   ¼ to ½ cup melted butter
- and then into   ½ cup sugar.

Crêpes

Method: grill.
Time: just until brown.
Yield: 12 to 16.

- Sift together

    1 cup sifted flour
    1 tablespoon sugar
    dash of salt.

- Combine

    1½ cups milk (or water)
    2 beaten eggs
    1 teaspoon lemon juice.

- Beat until smooth.
- Pour thin batter onto well-greased grill and spread until very thin.
- Turn when first side is brown and brown second side.

- Serve with one of the following,
  the crêpe either rolled or flat: jam
                                      cream cheese
                                      sour cream and
                                          powdered sugar

Variation: Serve with cheese or meats and vegetables in a white sauce.

Yeast Breads
Hot Rolls
Method: reflector oven, Dutch oven.
Time: three to four hours preparing; fifteen to twenty minutes cooking.
Yield: three to four dozen rolls.

■ Combine	2½ cups warm water
	2½ pkgs. yeast
	¼ cup butter
	3½ tablespoons sugar.
■ Sift (this can be done before going to camp)	7 cups flour
	2 teaspoons salt
	⅔ cup powdered milk.
■ Beat	3 eggs.
■ Make hole in dry ingredients and pour in all liquids.	
■ The dough will be very sticky; mix well and knead in	bowl.
■ Cover and set in warm place. Let rise until double in bulk.	
■ Punch down, take out of bowl, place on	floured surface.
■ Knead well.	
■ Shape into rolls and place in	buttered pan.
■ Let rise and bake.	

Variations:
- Cinnamon rolls: Double butter and sugar in recipe. Roll dough to ½-inch thickness. Brush with butter and sprinkle with 1 tablespoon sugar, 1 teaspoon cinnamon mixture. Sprinkle raisins on top. Roll up and cut into ½-inch-thick slices with string. Place in pan and bake after letting rise until doubled in size.

- Scones: Roll dough very thin with a can. Cut into pieces and make two or three holes in each piece. Fry in hot oil until golden brown.
- Stick bread: Roll dough into strips and mold around a stick which is about 1½ to 2 inches in diameter. Cook over hot coals.

Beverages

Mixes are best to use on cookouts because refrigeration is a problem. Remember that fresh milk sours quickly; so it is better to use powdered or canned milk with chocolate or use the chocolate mix recipe and add water as needed.

Care should be taken in using good water. If you are not sure the water is safe to use, bring your own from home or purify it by adding a few drops of chlorine bleach per gallon.

Hot Chocolate Mix

- Combine

1 8-qt. box powdered milk
1 16-oz. box instant chocolate
6 ozs. powdered cream
   substitute
2 cups powdered sugar.

- To prepare one cup of hot chocolate, use

3 tablespoons mix
1 cup hot water.

Pink Lemonade

- Mix well

1 pkg. pink lemonade Kool-aid
1 cup sugar
1½ qts. water.

- Chill.
- Just before serving, add

2 cups 7-Up or Sprite.

Punch Dandy

Yield: 5 gallons
- Combine

5 pkgs. orange Kool-aid
5 pkgs. cherry Kool-aid
10 cups sugar.

- Add

2 6-oz. cans frozen orange
   juice
2 cups pineapple juice
   (or 1 6-oz. can frozen
   pineapple juice).

- Mix together.

172

- Serve, using four parts water, one part mixture.

Almond Punch

■ Stir together	1 6-oz. can frozen orange juice
	1 6-oz. can frozen lemon juice
	1 cup sugar
	10 cups water
	1 teaspoon almond extract
	1 teaspoon vanilla.

- Chill and serve.

Desserts

A dessert can add that finish to a delicious outdoor meal. With a heavy meal, fruit may be all that is needed. With light meals serve heavier desserts. Do not be afraid to prepare favorite home-oven desserts since the Dutch oven can be used very effectively as an oven.

Fruit Kebab (colorplate 4)

Method: wire stick or spit.

Time: three to five minutes or until marshmallows are golden brown.

- Cut into one-inch sections   bananas.
- Prepare to place on skewer   chunk pineapple
  marshmallows
  maraschino cherries.
- Alternate items on skewer.
- Heat over coals until marsh-mallows are golden brown.

Variation: Other fruits such as strawberries, peaches, and plums can also be used.

Chocolate Pudding Cake

Methods: Dutch oven, reflector oven, can oven, pit.

Time: forty to fifty minutes.

Yield: 8 servings.

- Line inside of pan with   aluminum foil.
- Grease lightly with   butter.
- Mix   1 cup brown sugar
  ½ cup cocoa.
- Add and stir until blended   2 cups water.

173

- Add over the mixture
- Prepare and mix separately

1 cup miniature marshmallows.
1 devil's food cake mix
  (adjusted for altitude).

- Place pudding mixture in
  Dutch oven and spoon cake
  mix over the top.
- Top with

1 cup chopped nuts.

- Cover and bake.

Baked Apples
Method: wrapped in foil, Dutch oven, reflector oven, or can oven.
Time: forty-five to sixty minutes, until tender.
Yield: 4 apples.

- Core the center of

4 apples.

- Peel each apple about ⅓
  down.
- Place one of the following
  fillings in the center:

Filling 1
1 pkg. red hots.
Filling 2
brown sugar
marshmallows.
Filling 3
brown sugar
cinnamon
butter
nuts or raisins.

- Place each apple on a square
  of

aluminum foil.

- Bring foil up around sides and
  twist the top.
- Cook slowly.

Fruit Dumplings
Method: Dutch oven, reflector oven, can oven, or pit.
Time: twenty to thirty minutes or until brown.
Yield: 6 to 8 servings.

- Line inside of cooking pan with   aluminum foil.
- Put in cooking pan

2 #303 cans peaches (not
  juice).

- ■ Mix together and pour over fruit

  1 can juice

  1 tablespoon + 2 teaspoons cornstarch.

- ■ Dot with

  2 tablespoons butter

  ½ teaspoon nutmeg.

- ■ Place in or over coals to thicken and heat.
- ■ Mix until soft dough forms about consistency of muffins

  1 can juice

  Bisquick as needed.

- ■ When fruit mixture is hot, drop dough on top by spoonfuls.
- ■ Cover and bake.
- ■ Sprinkle and dot with

  3 tablespoons sugar

  1 tablespoon butter.

- ■ Cover and let sugar melt for two to three minutes to form a glaze over the cobbler.

Variations: Use other types of fruit; add cinnamon and sugar; use refrigerator biscuits cut in quarters.

Pioneer Cobbler

Method: Dutch oven, reflector oven, can ovens, or pit.

Time: twenty-five to thirty minutes, until brown.

Yield: 6 servings.

- ■ Line inside of cooking pan with

  aluminum foil.

- ■ Place in bottom of Dutch oven

  1 can or 1 quart peaches (sliced).

- ■ Sprinkle over top (may also be added to batter)

  1 teaspoon nutmeg

  1 to 2 tablespoons sugar.

- ■ Prepare and pour over top

  1 pkg. French vanilla or white cake mix adjusted for altitude.

- ■ Cover and cook.
- ■ Serve hot with whipped cream or pressurized canned cream.

Variation: applesauce, plums, or any fruit.

Fig. 153. Pineapple upside-down cake

Pineapple-upside-down Cake (fig. 153; colorplate 6)

Method: Dutch oven, can oven, tin can stove for miniature cakes, or can ovens.

Time: twenty-five to forty-five minutes, depending on heat.

Yield: 8 to 10 servings.

- Line cooking pan with   aluminum foil.
- Grease the pan with   oil or butter.
- Line the pan with   1 can pineapple slices.
- Sprinkle over pineapple   ½ cup brown sugar
                       2 to 3 tablespoons juice.

- Prepare and pour over fruit   1 white or yellow cake mix
                       (adjusted for altitude).

- Cover; place in heat.

Variations: other kinds of fruit; a maraschino cherry in each pineapple ring; different flavors of cake mixes; nuts.

Brown Bears in an Apple Orchard

Method: Dutch oven or reflector oven.

Time: twenty-five to forty-five minutes.

Yield: 8 to 9 servings.

- Line cooking pan with   aluminum foil.
- Grease the pan with   oil or butter.
- Line the bottom of the pan with   2 or 3 sliced apples.
- Mix and pour over fruit   1 pkg. gingerbread mix.
- Cover.
- Place in heat.

Cake in an Orange (colorplate 7)

Method: Place in coals, reflector oven, or Dutch oven.
Time: ten to fifteen minutes.
Yield: 10 to 12 servings.
- Mix   1 cake mix and ingredients.
- Slice off ⅓ down from top   10 to 12 oranges.
- Spoon fruit out of bottom
  two-thirds, leaving an empty
  shell.
- Fill the hollow shell ½ full with
  cake batter. Place lid back on
  orange.
- If available, wrap orange in   6″ × 6″ piece of foil.
- Place in heat.

Variations: gingerbread mix; grapefruit shell.

Cherry Delight (colorplate 7)

Method: Dutch oven
Time: twenty to thirty minutes
- Line Dutch oven with   aluminum foil.
- Place in Dutch oven   1 large can pie cherry filling.
- Sprinkle over pie filling   half box of dry cake mix.
- Place coals under and on top
  of Dutch oven, bake until crust
  is golden brown.

Variations: other fruit fillings.

Graham Cracker Cherry Pudding

Method: Dutch oven, reflector oven, can oven, or pit.
Time: twenty to thirty minutes, until warmed through.
Yield: 8 to 9 servings.
- Line cooking pan with   aluminum foil.
- Combine   20 graham crackers
                                                            ¼ cup butter
                                                            ½ cup chopped nuts
                                                            2 tablespoons sugar.

- Butter aluminum foil.
- Sprinkle ⅔ of graham cracker
  mixture on bottom.
- Cover with   1 can cherry pie filling.

- Sprinkle remaining graham cracker mix over top.
- Cover and bake.

Variations: other fruits; half a package of cake mix powder sprinkled over top of fruit.

Easy Brownies

Method: reflector oven, can oven, or Dutch oven.

Time: thirty to forty minutes, just until done.

Yield: 24 brownies.

- Line inside of cooking pan with aluminum foil.
- Mix together and beat
  - 1½ cups flour
  - 2 cups sugar
  - ½ cup + 2 tablespoons cocoa
  - 1 teaspoon salt
  - 1 cup oil
  - 4 eggs
  - 1 teaspoon vanilla
  - ½ cup nuts.

- Spoon into pan.
- Cook until done.

Snacks

Probably some of the best memories of camp come from cooking those ever-popular snack items: s'mores or banana boats. Some snack items should be included with each daily menu as an energy item on a hike, as an extra treat, or as a campfire addition. The following are only the beginning of good things for snacks in the out-of-doors.

Fig. 154. S'mores

178

S'mores (fig. 154)

Method: stick, reflector oven.

Time: two or three minutes, until marshmallow is golden brown.

- Toast over coals on a stick   2 marshmallows.
- Place on bottom   1 graham cracker square
  1 chocolate square .

- Place toasted marshmallows on chocolate square.
- Place on top   1 graham cracker square.

Hint: Chocolate will melt better if placed in center of marshmallow.

Variations: Make filling out of peanut butter and jam instead of chocolate. Cook in reflector oven: graham cracker on bottom, marshmallows and filling. When marshmallows are golden brown, place graham cracker on top.

Banana Boat (fig. 155)

Method: foil.

Time: five minutes.

- Cut wedge-shaped section in   banana.
- Remove wedge.
- Place in hollow left in banana   marshmallows
  chocolate chips.

- Cover marshmallow with peeled-back banana skin and wrap in   aluminum foil.
- Place in coals until chocolate and marshmallows are heated.

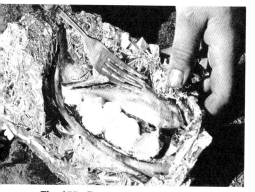

Fig. 155. Banana boat

179

No-cook Fudge

- Blend together   ¼ cup cocoa
scant square butter (soft)
¼ lb. grated cheese
(room temperature).

- Add   1 lb. powdered sugar
¼ cup chopped nuts
1 tablespoon vanilla.

- Mix thoroughly.
- Shape into long rolls; put in   waxed paper.
- Let set and slice.

No-bake Cookies

Method: kettle over coals.
Time: until liquid ingredients boil.
Yield: 3 to 4 dozen.

- Prepare sheet with   waxed paper or foil.
- Mix together and boil   2 cups sugar
½ cup milk
½ cup shortening
3 tablespoons cocoa
½ teaspoon salt.

- Add to mixture   3 cups quick oats (instant)
½ cup nuts
1 cup coconut
1 teaspoon vanilla.

- Drop by spoonfuls on sheet.
Leave until cool and set up.

Shaggy Dogs (fig. 156)

Method: stick.
Time: three minutes.

- Heat in the can   1 can chocolate syrup.
- Toast until golden brown   1 package marshmallows.
- Dip marshmallows in
chocolate syrup and roll in   1 package coconut.

Outdoor Chocolate Cones (fig. 157)

- Mix as directed on package   1 package chocolate cake mix.
- Serve in   ice cream cones (or dishes).

Variation: Use a commercial instant pudding mix. Top with whip cream or substitute.

180

Fig. 156. Shaggy dog

Fig. 157. Outdoor pudding cone

Gorp

■ Combine

1 package of sugared cereal
2 cups M&Ms
2 cups salted nuts
2 cups raisins.

Hint: This is great to package and take on hikes.

Fig. 158. Plastic sourdough container

SOURDOUGH BREAD

Delicious sourdough bread, so popular with today's woodsmen, miners, fishermen, and hunters, was the principal bread of the hardworking men who built the West. You can enjoy its heartiness and flavor, too (colorplate 8).

Description

Sourdough is developed from a culture of flour, water, and wild yeast. This wild yeast is atmospheric bacteria, similar to the bacteria in souring milk or other souring foods. The bread and hotcakes are developed from what is commonly called a starter. It is from the starter that dough is taken for use. Some dough is always left over (about one to two cups) to activate new dough; this is called the starter.

Although in the past it has been supposed that the starters brought from the old country or used over long periods are superior to newly developed starters, this is not true. Well-developed new starters may produce a product comparable to the older ones.

Container

The most common sourdough container for camp or home use is an earthenware crock (with a loose-fitting lid) with a one- to two-gallon capacity. Plastic or other nonmetallic containers with loose-fitting lids are equally satisfactory (fig. 158). Acids from the bacterial action of the dough act on metal; so metal containers should not be used. It is essential that the lid or cover is loose or not sealed, as it may explode if the gas cannot escape.

Making the Sourdough Starter

Starting methods vary. However, the following method works well:

- In a crock or plastic container place

  1 cup flour
  ½ yeast cake or
  ½ pkg. dry yeast
  1 teaspoon sugar.
  about 1½ cups warm water

- Add and mix into a thick batter

  or

- Add, if desired (with or instead of water)

  1½ cups milk, buttermilk, or yogurt, or perhaps potato water with or without sugar.

- Each day for two to three days add and mix to a thick batter

  1 cup fresh flour
  warm water.

- Let set for one to three days until the batter becomes a good, active starter.
- After the starter is working well, mix the amount of dough you need by adding

  flour and water.

- Take out what you need, leaving sufficient dough to retain a starter (one to two cups).

Maintaining Sourdough Starter

To maintain a good starter, you should use the dough frequently, preferably daily. You can maintain the starter over several days or weeks, however, by refrigerating or freezing it. To do so, refrigerate or freeze the starter prior to mixing it for a new batch of bread or hotcakes. Remove it from the refrigerator or freezer a day or so before using it and permit the starter to warm and reactivate at a warm (not hot) temperature. To shorten the rising time, mix the dough with warm water and keep it in a warm place; do not use hot water. To lengthen the rising time, mix the dough with cold water and keep it in a cool place.

In outdoor camps during cold periods the dough can be mixed with warm water and covered with insulation such as coats or bedding, or it may be kept in an insulated box. During warm weather mix it with cold water and keep it in a cool place. If the dough gets too sour, it will not make a good product and must be poured out, except for a sufficient amount to activate a new starter. Adding cultured yeast helps to regenerate the starter. When you are mixing the dough, the container should be less than half full at first because otherwise it will more than double in size and overflow the container.

Sourdough for Bread and Biscuits
General procedure
After the starter is working well, add flour and water to it to make the amount of sourdough sufficient for your needs. (Remember to leave one or two cups for maintaining the starter.) The amount of dough you mix will depend on the number of loaves or biscuits desired. The dough in the starter mix should be prepared the night before or several hours prior to making bread or biscuits. A good, active starter dough will more than double its volume and will become bubbly. The bubbles are created by gas given off by the action of the yeast.

Sourdough loaf bread and biscuits can be made in the same way with slight variations. The dough for loaf bread should be mixed so it is stiffer, left to rise longer, and baked longer than that for biscuits.

Mixing bread and biscuits
The old-time method for mixing bread is to place flour in a deep kettle and with the back of the fingers press it out into a bowl shape. Into this bowl-shaped flour, pour the desired amount of activated, raw sourdough. Remember to leave sufficient (one to two cups) in the container to restart the next batch.

When old-timers were "packing," they would carry flour in a seamless sack or a heavy flour sack, roll the top of the sack back to the level of the flour, shape the flour in the top of the sack with their fingers into a bowl shape, pour dough into the bowl-shaped flour, and mix it (fig. 159).

■Recipes for good sourdough vary greatly. However, the following proportions may be used as a guide.
- In a flour-lined pan or sack,
  place   2 cups sourdough.
- Add   ½ teaspoon salt
                                          1 teaspoon baking powder.

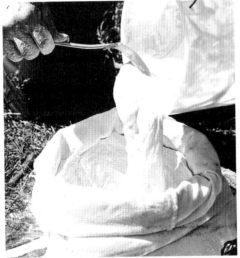
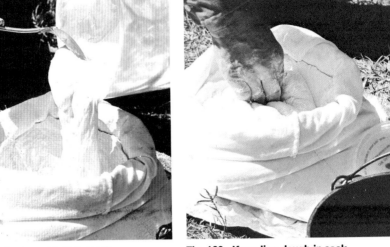

Fig. 159. Mixing bread in flour sack   **Fig. 160. Kneading dough in sack**

- Add, depending on how sour the dough is (if it is not too sour, baking soda may be eliminated when using baking powder), about —   ¼ teaspoon baking soda.
- Add as desired   2 to 4 tablespoons shortening or bacon grease.
- Add if desired (not necessary)   1 to 2 tablespoons sugar.
- Knead thoroughly by mixing the dough into the flour from the outside to the center (fig. 160). Loaf bread dough should be stiffer than biscuit dough. Form into loaves or biscuits, turn in a greased pan, or brush top with shortening or oil.
- Let rise to about double its original size (time varies according to temperature).
- Bake: Biscuits twenty to thirty minutes in oven 375 to 400°.
    Loaf bread about one hour in oven 350 to 375°.
- After baking the bread or biscuits, oil or grease the top, cover with cloth, and keep warm if desired.

Sourdough Hotcakes (colorplate 2)

General procedure

Sourdough for hotcakes is prepared as it is for loaf bread or biscuits, except that the starter should be thinner.

Pour sufficient activated dough into a pan or mixing bowl; add at least one egg per person; bacon grease, melted shortening, or cooking oil; salt; and sugar. Mix ingredients and thin them with canned (condensed) milk. When the batter is mixed to the desired consistency, add baking bowder and/or baking soda and cook on a hot grill. Improve the texture by using one-half to equal parts of prepared hotcake mix and sourdough and still retain the delicious sourdough flavor.

Specific proportions and procedures

In mountain use, each man generally developed his own recipes and nothing was measured. Recipes that exist vary greatly. However, the following proportions may aid the beginner. Practice develops a good hotcake maker.

- Place in a mixing bowl
  1 cup sourdough.
- Add
  ½ to 1 cup prepared hotcake mix

  1 to 2 eggs

  1 teaspoon salt

  2 to 3 tablespoons melted shortening, cooking oil, or bacon grease (bacon grease improves the flavor)

  1 tablespoon sugar (Add more or less sugar to get a darker or lighter brown color).

- As the ingredients are mixed, thin the mixture with
  Condensed (canned) milk or whole or skimmed milk.

- After a medium batter is obtained, add
  1 teaspoon baking powder.

- Add (according to the sourness of the dough)
  ¼ (or less) teaspoon baking soda (Leave out if dough is not very sour).

One of the essentials in making good hotcakes is cooking them on a hot grill. The grill should smoke when greased or oiled, and it should sizzle if water is dropped on it. Try making a small sample cake to see if it turns golden brown instead of a light brown or whitish color. A grill which is not hot enough will not make good cakes, and if it is too hot, it will burn them. A heavy aluminum or iron grill, a Dutch oven, or a Dutch oven lid will produce pleasing results.

Eat the hotcakes as they are taken from the grill. The quality cannot be maintained if they are stacked or allowed to stand.

FIRST AID

The first consideration on any camping trip should be safety measures that will prevent illness and accident. Remember that the best first aid is preventive first aid. For general safety rules, consider the following suggestions:

- Don't overdo physical activity.
- Avoid too much sun.
- Don't let yourself become exhausted or overtired.
- Know *how* to use tools before using them.
- Maintain safe and protected places for tools.
- When necessary, use insect repellent.
- Purify the water.
- Watch where you step; don't try to travel too fast.
- Keep away from dangerous places such as steep ledges, mines, or caves, and slopes covered with loose rocks.
- Practice good sanitation habits; provide several places to wash hands.
- Use a good detergent and clean water to wash dishes. If there is any question about the sanitation of the water, dip dishes in boiling sterile water. Be sure to rinse all soap off dishes.
- Do not drink out of a community canteen.
- When hiking or mountain climbing use proper equipment, including good, sturdy shoes.
- Wear adequate clothing that will maintain protection from sun, wind, cold, or heat.

When problems do occur requiring first aid, remember that you are a first-aider, not a doctor. Serious problems must be handled by a physician. First aid is, to a great degree, just plain common sense. Do not "overdo" your treatment. More damage and injury to an individual may be done by an untrained or too-enthusiastic first-aider than by leaving the victim entirely alone. The following brief definitions and treatments are not intended to be comprehensive. They are a simple summary of some first-aid problems you may encounter. (For a good, up-to-date treatment of first aid, obtain a copy of the American National Red Cross's *First Aid and*

Personal Safety. Be sure to get the *most recent issue.*) Use the following suggestions as a guide only.

Definitions and Treatments
Artificial respiration

A respiratory emergency is one in which normal breathing stops or slows to a point insufficient to sustain life. The most obvious sign is, of course, that the breathing movements have stopped. The victim turns blue.

Treatment: Mouth-to-mouth artificial respiration is the most practical method for getting someone to start breathing again. Wipe any visible foreign matter from the victim's mouth quickly and tilt his head backward so that his chin is pointing upward. Maintain this position throughout the entire resuscitation time. Pinch the nostrils closed with thumb and forefinger. Blow a deep breath into the victim's mouth after sealing your mouth around his (fig. 161).

See that the chest rises. Turn your head to the side and listen for the return breath. Make sure the chest falls. Repeat the blowing cycle twelve to eighteen times per minute for an adult.

When you are giving artificial respiration to a small child, use puffs of air rather than big breaths to avoid damage to the lungs. A child breathes at a faster rate (twenty times per minute) than an adult.

Fig. 161. Mouth-to-mouth artificial respiration

190

If the stomach bulges, put pressure on it to release the trapped air. This may cause regurgitation. If so, turn the patient to the side so that he does not swallow the regurgitated matter, clean the mouth again, and start the process over.

A number of people breathe through an opening in the neck (a stoma) rather than through the nose or mouth. In this case mouth-to-stoma resuscitation would be necessary since air blown in the mouth would never reach the lungs.

Breathe for the patient until he breathes regularly for himself or until he is pronounced dead by a doctor.

As the patient begins to breathe for himself, his breath will be somewhat irregular and gasping. Try to breathe air into him each time he struggles for it.

Bleeding wounds

Abrasion or scratch. The skin is scraped, rubbed, or scratched, causing a burning surface pain. The area is prone to infection if not cleaned thoroughly.

Treatment: Wash the area with soap and water, using gauze and washing away from the wound. Apply a sterile dressing. Do not touch the side of the dressing which goes next to the wound. Seek medical attention.

Lacerated wound. The skin is torn or crushed, causing slight bleeding. The area is predisposed to infection.

Treatment: Treatment is the same as for abrasion or scratch.

Incised wound. The skin is broken by a sharp instrument. Because these wounds bleed freely, they are less likely to develop infection. Deep cuts may damage muscles, tendons, and nerves.

Treatment: Control the bleeding. Follow abrasion treatment. If bleeding is difficult to control, don't attempt to clean the wound. Secure the dressing and take the victim directly to a physician.

Puncture wound. The tissue is penetrated deeply by a pointed object such as a nail or a fish hook. There is little surface injury, though internal damage may cause internal bleeding.

Treatment: Stimulate bleeding and then follow abrasion treatment. In puncture wounds the danger of tetanus is great. Always consult a physician for treatment.

Severe bleeding

External hemorrhage (bleeding) from severe wounds may be treated. Internal hemorrhage must be treated by a physician.

Treatment: Keep the victim lying down to prevent fainting and to control shock. Elevate the bleeding part unless there is evidence of a fracture. Techniques to stop severe bleeding are described in order of preference.

Direct pressure.   Apply pressure to the wound with your bare hand, if necessary, until a dressing can be used. If blood saturates the gauze, apply additional layers and continue the pressure.

Pressure on the supplying artery.   If the use of a pressure point should be necessary, use it in conjunction with direct pressure and elevation of the wound. There are only two pressure points worth considering here. Use the brachial artery for the control of severe bleeding from an open arm wound. This pressure point is located on the inside of the arm about midway between the armpit and the elbow. To apply pressure on the brachial artery, grasp the middle of the victim's upper arm, your thumb on the outside of his arm and your fingers on the inside. Press your fingers toward your thumb to create an inward force from opposite sides of the arm. Use the flat, inside surface of your finger, not your fingertips. This inward pressure holds and closes the artery by compressing it against the arm bone (fig. 162).

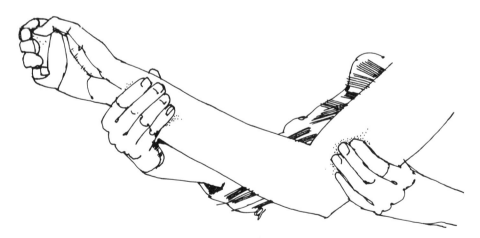

Fig. 162. Applying pressure on the brachial artery

Use the femoral artery for the control of severe bleeding from an open leg wound. This pressure point is located just below the groin on the front, inner half of the thigh (fig. 163). To apply pressure, position the victim flat on his back, if possible, and place the heel of your hand directly over the pressure point.

The tourniquet. The use of a tourniquet to control bleeding is justifiable only on rare occasions. You risk the sacrifice of a limb. Place the tourniquet just above the wound, not allowing it to touch the wound. If the wound is at a joint, place the tourniquet above the joint. Wrap the tourniquet band (at least two inches wide) tightly around the limb twice and tie a half knot. Place a short, strong stick or other similar object on the knot and tie two additional overhand knots on top of the stick. Twist the stick to tighten the tourniquet until the bleeding stops. Secure the stick so that it will not become loose. Record time and place of tourniquet and attach it to the victim. *Do not loosen* the tourniquet except on the advice of the attending physician.

Blisters

Friction, pinching, or local irritation may cause the skin or the flesh under the skin to redden or rise, resulting in a blister.

Treatment: If the blister is likely to become broken, cleanse the surrounding area with soap and water. Sterilize a needle by passing it through the flame of a match several times. Puncture

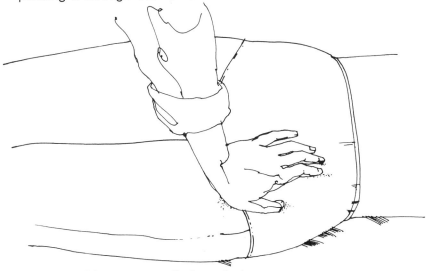

Fig. 163. Applying pressure on the femoral artery

the blister at its edge and apply gentle pressure to its outside margin. Apply a sterile dressing to protect the area from further irritation. If the blister is extensive or infection is present, consult a physician.

Bone fractures

A fracture is a break or a crack in a bone which may be either closed (the break cannot be seen externally) or open (bones protrude through a break in the skin). The victim may be able to provide clues to his condition such as "feeling" the bone snap, hearing or feeling a grating sensation. Other signs include obvious deformities, swelling, discoloration, pain, or tenderness to touch.

Treatment: Whenever a fracture is suspected, treat as for a fracture. If medical attention can be obtained in a reasonable amount of time, do not attempt to set a fracture or to push a protruding bone end back.

Do not move the victim unless there is a chance of further injury if you don't. (If there is bleeding, treat for bleeding.) Prevent motion of the injured parts. Treat for shock. (Do not lift limbs suspected of being broken.) If the victim must be moved, wait for adequate help, especially if there is a chance of back or neck fractures. Immobilizing fractures should be done by trained first-aiders or rescue squads. If help will be unavailable for a long period of time, a simple splinting procedure might include taping or tying an injured leg to the uninjured one — with padding between, if possible — or binding an injured arm (after padding it) to the chest if the elbow is bent or to the side if the elbow is straight. Make sure splints are long enough to extend beyond the joints above and below the fracture. Check periodically to make sure there is no undue swelling or color change and that numbness does not result from tying or taping that is too tight.

Sprains

Swelling, tenderness, and pain while the joint is in motion are the symptoms of sprains. Sometimes the skin discolors over a large area. The degree of swelling or pain does not distinguish a sprain from a fracture.

Treatment: If there is a possibility of a fracture, immobilize the part as in treatment of a fracture. Otherwise, elevate the joint on pillows or their substitutes. Cold, wet applications or an ice bag during the first half hour after the injury may retard the swelling.

Thereafter, cold packs may be applied as needed. Keep the joint immobilized. Have the sprain x-rayed.

Strains

Strains are injuries to muscles from overexertion.

Treatment: Apply heat and warm, wet applications, and rest. If the back is strained, use a board under the mattress.

Burns

Chemical burns. Irritating chemicals destroy skin cells. Treatment should begin immediately.

Treatment: Flood the burned area gently with copius amounts of water for at least five minutes. If first-aid directions for burns caused by specific chemicals are available, follow those directions AFTER the initial flushing with water. Apply a dressing, and seek medical attention.

First-degree or minor burns. These are characterized by reddening of the skin, mild swelling, and pain. Sunburn and overexposure to ultra-violet rays are good examples.

Treatment: Using cold water on first-degree burns for at least fifteen minutes may prevent blisters from forming. If a first-degree burn covers a large area of skin, the patient may become nauseous and may experience chilling or extreme pain. Make the patient as comfortable as possible. Seek medical attention.

Second-degree burns. Second-degree burns form blisters.

Treatment: Submerge the burned area in cold water for one to two hours to stop tissue damage. Apply clean, cold cloths and blot dry gently. Cover the burn with a thick pad of sterile dry dressings.

Never apply oil, antiseptics, or burn ointments to an extensive burn.

Third-degree burns. These burns are characterized by a white or charcoal appearance. The cells that form new skin are destroyed because the burn has extended through all skin layers. Third-degree burns are generally not as painful as first- and second-degree burns since the nerve endings in the skin have been destroyed.

Treatment: Cut clothing away from the burned areas. If cloth adheres to the burn, cut gently around it, not attempting to remove it. Cover the burn with thick sterile dressings or clean cloths. Keep the burned area elevated. Treat for shock.

Again, do not apply ointments, commercial preparations, grease, or other home remedies.

Fainting

Fainting is a partial or complete loss of consciousness due to a reduced supply of blood to the brain, recognizable by paleness, sweating, dizziness, and sometimes nausea.

Treatment: Have the person lie down with his head lower than his feet.   Loosen constricting bands of clothing, and increase ventilation in the room.   Examine the victim to determine whether or not he has suffered injury from falling.   If symptoms of fainting occur with the victim in a sitting position, prevent his fainting by bending him over and placing his head between his knees for a few minutes.

Heat

Heat exhaustion.   In mild cases too much sun will cause exhaustion, headache, and nausea.   The face will be pale with cold sweat on the forehead.   In more serious cases, there will be a lot of perspiration; the body will feel clammy.   Although there will not be a fever, there may be vomiting and slow breathing.

Treatment: Have the victim lie in a shady spot.   Bed rest in a cool room is better.   Keep the head lower than the feet.   Give sips of salt water — one teaspoon of salt to a glass of water (half a glass every fifteen minutes).   If the patient is vomiting do not give further fluids.   If symptoms continue to be serious, call a doctor.

Heat and sun stroke.   A significant warning of extreme exposure to the sun or very hot weather is a lack of perspiration which will cause high body temperature.   The skin is hot, red, and dry.   Other signs may be nausea, dizziness, fast, strong pulse, and headache.   The victim may lose consciousness.

Treatment: In heat stroke it is vital to get the temperature down immediately since high, sustained temperatures may cause permanent brain damage.   Medical attention and perhaps hospitalization will be necessary, but until they are available, keep the victim lying down out of the sun and heat.   Give repeated sponge baths with water or rubbing alcohol to reduce the body temperature, or apply cold packs continuously.   Or place the victim in a tub of cold water (do not add ice) until his temperature is lowered sufficiently.   When the temperature is down, dry him off but repeat the process if the temperature begins to rise.   Do not give stimulants.

Insect bites.

Most insects inject an acid when they bite.

Treatment: For minor bites and stings, cold applications and soothing lotions may be all that is necessary. Carefully, with tweezers or a gentle massaging action, remove the stinger if it is still in the wound, taking care not to break the venom sac. Apply alcohol or baking soda paste. Avoid scratching; it may cause infection. Some people are hyperallergic to ant, bee, hornet, or wasp stings. If allergy signs appear, get the victim to a doctor immediately, as death may result. In the meantime for these and more serious bites, apply a constricting band above the injection site on the victim's arm or leg between the site and the heart. Do not apply tightly. Keep the affected part of the body below the level of the heart. Apply ice packs or cold cloths to the site of the wound.

Tick bites

Ticks are brown, flat, round insects about ¼ inch long with eight legs. They may be infected with disease-producing organisms.

Treatment: Cover the tick with heavy oil to close its breathing pores. If it doesn't disengage at once, allow the oil to remain in place for half an hour. If the tick doesn't disengage, carefully remove it with tweezers. Take the time necessary to remove all parts of it. Scrub the area thoroughly with soap and water. Never touch the tick with your hands. This prevents the spread of disease-producing germs.

Poison oak, ivy, and sumac

Itching, redness, rashes, blistering, and general symptoms of headache and fever may accompany plant poisoning. Learn to identify the plants and avoid them. Smoke from burning these plants may also be irritating.

Treatment: As soon as possible, remove contaminated clothing and wash the exposed areas with a thick lather of soap and water. Rinse many times. Do not use a brush, as this may introduce the irritating substance more deeply into the tissues. Apply calamine lotion to soothe the itching. Seek medical advice if a severe reaction occurs.

Poisonous snakebite

Quick action is necessary. Poison must be removed as soon as possible. The best treatment for snakebites by the untrained first-aider is as follows:

- Stop all muscular activity and calm the victim, taking care to keep the wound lower than the heart.
- Place a constricting band above the bite between the wound and the heart.
- Apply cold packs to slow distribution of venom.
- Get medical attention quickly.

If you have a snakebite kit, you may use it. Follow the instructions given in the kit. Great care and caution must be exercised by a first-aider attempting to make incisions over a snake bite; the consequences may be far worse than the bite itself.

Shock

Shock is a depressed state of many vital functions. The skin is pale, moist, and cool. Cold perspiration forms on the forehead, palms, and armpits. The pulse and respiration are weak and rapid. Frequently there is nausea and vomiting. Pupils may be dilated. The person may become progressively weaker and incoherent.

Treatment: Keep the victim lying down. Reassure him and make him comfortable. Move him as little as possible, changing his position only if you have safely determined that there are no broken bones. Lower the head and shoulders and raise the legs. If there is a head wound, the head should be level with the body or slightly elevated.

Maintain body temperature. If medical attention is slow in arriving, give fluids — preferably the saline solution (one teaspoon salt and ½ teaspoon baking soda to one quart of water) — if the person is conscious and not nauseated. Do not give fluids if there are abdominal injuries. Do not give stimulating drinks.

With shock, psychology is important. A great deal of the treatment of shock may depend on the reactions of others. Strong reassurance that there is nothing to worry about and that others involved in the accident or mishap are being cared for is the best approach. If onlookers are overly curious, hysterical, or unwise in what they say, they may cause a deeper shock, which may cause death — even when the wounds themselves do not justify it. Shock may also be a delayed reaction; be prepared to treat shock even hours after the accident.

INDEX

A

Abrasion 191
A-frame 44
Aluminum foil
    cooking with 69-73
    wrapping food with 70, 73
Apples, baked 174
Artificial respiration 190-91
Ash cakes 106

B

Backpacker's oven 113
Bac-o-cheese dogs 137
Bacon and egg in a sack 132
Bacon on a stick 132
Banana boat 179
Barbecue, can 75-76
Basic Four Food Groups 115
Bathtub 37
Beans
    baked 161-62
    hot pot green 160
    New England baked 162
Bedroll 7
Beef stroganoff 145
Bench, log 29
Beverages 172-73
Biscuits
    sourdough 185-86
    stick 167
Biscuits supreme 165
Bites
    insect 197
    snake 198
    tick 197
Bleeding, severe 192-93
Bleeding, stoppage of 192-93
    by direct pressure 192

by pressure on supplying
    artery 192-93
    by tourniquet 193
Bleeding wounds 191
Blisters 193-94
Bone fractures 194
Bread cup on a stick 169
Bread
    dough boy 169
    Indian fry 169
    sourdough 185-86
    stick 172
    thumbprint 167
Breads 165-72
    quick 165-71
    yeast 171-72
Bread twist 166-69
Breakfast, overnight 133
Brown bears in an apple orchard
    176
Brownies, easy 178
Bunyon burger 140
Burns 195-96
    chemical 195
    first-degree 195
    second-degree 195
    third-degree 195-96

C

Cake
    chocolate pudding 173-74
    in an orange 177
    pineapple-upside-down
        176
Campfire sandwich 135
Camping equipment list, general
    13
Cannonballs 140
Casserole, quick macaroni 146

Cereal   132
Charcoal briquets   51-52
Checklist for food   121-22
Chemical burns   195
Cherry delight   177
Chicken dinner, Dutch oven   148
Chicken dinners   148, 157
Chicken in Dutch oven   148
Chicken in pit   157
Chicken on a spit   157
Chili, camp   161
Chocolate, hot   172
Cinnamon rolls   171
Cinnamon toast   133
Cobbler, pioneer   175
Cole slaw   164
Cookies, no-bake   180
Cooking
    aluminum foil   69-73
    in paper bag   103
    in paper cup   103
    in sand   109
    nonutensil   102-5
    on manifold of car   111-13
    pit   98-101
    rock   107
    spit   57, 59, 61
    stick   57, 59, 61
Cooking equipment, improvised
    10-12
Cooking time chart   124-26
Cooking without recipes   128
Corn on the cob   160
Crêpes   170-71
Crisscross fire   44

D

Desserts, 173-78. *See also* Snacks
    baked apples   174
    brown bears in an apple
        orchard   176
    cake in an orange   177
    cherry delight   177
    chocolate pudding cake
        173-74

easy brownies   178
fruit dumplings   174-75
fruit kebab   173
graham cracker cherry
    pudding   177-78
pineapple-upside-down
    cake   176
pioneer cobbler   175
Dingle fan roaster   109-10
Doughnuts
    twisted   170
    holes   170
Double boiler   109
Dough boy   169
Dumplings, fruit   174-75
Dutch oven   82-92

E

Eggs
    creamed   130
    fried   129
    poached   130
    scrambled   130
    soft and hard cooked   129
    white sauce   129
Eggs in a basket   130
Eggs in a sack   132
Equipment list, personal   8-9

F

Fainting   196
Fire
    crisscross   44
    Indian   44
    keyhole   22
    log cabin   44
    star   44
    teepee   44
    trench   23
    methods of starting   46
    types of   44
First-degree burns   195
Fish, baked   158
Fish dinners   157-58

Fish
 fried 157
 steamed 158
Foil dinner 143
Food, checklist for 121-22
Food storage 23, 27
Food substitutes 127
Fractures, bone 194
Frank-a-bobs 138
French toast 134
Fudge, no-cook 180
Fuel 42

G

Gorp 181

H

Hamburger, basic mix 139
Hamburger stew 144
Heat exhaustion 196
Heat stroke 196
Heat tablets 50
Hemorrhage 192
Hotcakes, sourdough 187-88
Hot chocolate mix 172
Hot-water tank, outdoor 29

I

Indian fire 44
Insect bites 197
Ivy, poison 197

J

Jello salad 164

K

Keyhole fire 22
Kindling 42

L

Lantern 10
Latrine 37
Lemonade, pink 172
Log cabin fire 44
Lunch, no-fuss 136

M

Macaroni, quick, casserole 146
Master Planning Chart 17-20
Meal planner, three-day 117
Meat loaf 140
 miniature, in cabbage leaves
  142
 on a stick 139
 quick 141
Minute pizza 135
Muffins 166

N

No-fuss lunch 136
Nonutensil cooking 102-5

O

Oak, poison 197
Oil drum stove 111
Outdoor chocolate cones 180
Oven
 backpacker's 113
 Dutch 82-92
 reflector 92-98
Ovens, can 78-82
Overnight breakfast 133

P

Pancakes 133
Paper bag, cooking in 103
Paper cup, cooking in 103
Personal equipment list 8-9
Pig in a blanket 136
Pit cooking 98-101
Pizza 135
 minute 135
Planning chart, master 17-20
Poison ivy 197
Poison oak 197
Poison sumac 197
Pork chops, stuffed 147
Potato, Swiss 160
Potatoes
 baked 159
 boiled 159

fried   159
   scalloped   159-60
Punch, almond   173
Punch, dandy   172-73
Pudding, graham cracker cherry
   177-78

R

Reflector oven   92-98
Refrigerators, outdoor   23-26
Roaster, dingle fan   109-10
Rock cooking   107
Roesti (Swiss potato)   160
Rolls
   cinnamon   171
   hot   171

S

Safety rules   189
Salads   162-65
   cole slaw   164
   German potato   163-64
   jello   164
   macaroni   162-63
   potato   163
   tossed green   162
   Waldorf   164-65
   watermelon   165
Sandwich, campfire   135
Scones   172
Scratches   191
Second-degree burns   195
Shaggy dogs   180
Shish kebab   146
Shock   198
Shopping guide   118-20
Shower   37
Sloppy joes   135
S'mores   179
Snacks   178-81. See also
   Desserts
   banana boat   179
   gorp   181
   no-bake cookies   180
   no-cook fudge   180

outdoor chocolate cones
   180
   shaggy dogs   180
   s'mores   179   ·
Snakebite   198
Sourdough
   biscuits   185-86
   bread   185-86
   bread starter   183, 184-85
   hotcakes   187-88
Spareribs, barbecued   147
Spit cooking   57, 59, 61
Sprains   194-95
Star fire   44
Starter   183, 184-85
Stew, camp   147
Stew
   hamburger   144
   special   134
Stick cooking   57, 59, 61
Storage
   equipment   32-33
   food   23, 27
Stove
   oil drum   111
   tall can   73-74
   tin can   62-68
Strains   195
Sumac, poison   197
Sun stroke   196

T

Tacos   144
Teepee fire   44
Three-day Meal Planner   117
Third-degree burns   195-96
Tick bites   197
Tinder   42
Toast   106
   cinnamon   133
   French   134
Toastite   110
Toilet, portable   39
Tomatoes, fried   161
Trench fire   23

V

Vegetables   158-59
    canned   158
    fresh   158
    in foil   159

W

Wound
    incised   191
    lacerated   191
    puncture   191
Wounds, bleeding   191

Z

Zucchini, stuffed   142